Oxford International Resources

8

T0369597

English
Student Book

Emma Danihel
Rachel Redford

OXFORD

OXFORD
UNIVERSITY PRESS

Great Clarendon Street, Oxford, OX2 6DP, United Kingdom

Oxford University Press is a department of the University of Oxford.
It furthers the University's objective of excellence in research, scholarship, and education by publishing worldwide. Oxford is a registered trade mark of Oxford University Press in the UK and in certain other countries.

First published in 2023

British Library Cataloguing in Publication Data

Data available

ISBN 978-1-38-203600-9

10 9 8 7 6 5 4 3 2

MIX
Paper | Supporting responsible forestry
FSC www.fsc.org FSC® C007785

The manufacturing process conforms to the environmental regulations of the country of origin.

Printed in the UK by Bell and Bain Ltd, Glasgow

Acknowledgements

The publisher and authors would like to thank the following for permission to use photographs and other copyright material:

Cover: Dan Gartman. Photos: **p4(t):** Frank Fennema/Shutterstock; **p4(b):** Andrey Pavlov/Shutterstock; **p5:** Stephen Finn/Shutterstock; **p7:** photo.ua/Shutterstock; **p8:** Stanick/Shutterstock; **p9(t):** Xinhua / Alamy Stock Photo; **p9(b):** Mikhail Rulkov/Shutterstock; **pp10-11(1):** Digital Vision/Getty Images; **pp10-11(2):** Jon Arnold Images Ltd / Alamy Stock Photo; **pp10-11(3):** Clara/Shutterstock; **pp10-11(4):** Edwin Remsberg / Alamy Stock Photo; **pp10-11(5):** Amra Pasic/Shutterstock; **pp10-11(6):** guichaoua / Alamy Stock Photo; **pp10-11(7):** Margouillat/Dreamstime; **pp10-11(8):** Pavol Kmeto/Shutterstock; **pp10-11(9):** Powered by Light/Alan Spencer / Alamy Stock Photo; **p12:** PHB.cz (Richard Semik)/Shutterstock; **p14:** Seva_blsv/Shutterstock; **p17:** Alessia Pierdomenico/Shutterstock; **p20:** P.KASIPAT/Shutterstock; **p21:** Tony Vaccaro/Hulton Archive/Getty Images; **p22:** INTERFOTO / Alamy Stock Photo; **p24(t):** Betsy Streeter/Cartoonstock; **p24(b):** Ellis Rosen/Cartoonstock; **p25:** Grafinger/Shutterstock; **p26:** Science History Images / Alamy Stock Photo; **p29(t):** pryzmat / Shutterstock; **p29(b):** VectorPlotnikoff/Shutterstock; **p31:** Brand X Pictures/Getty Images; **p32:** wavebreakmedia/Shutterstock; **p34:** Hemis / Alamy Stock Photo; **p36:** Photodisc / Getty Images; **p37:** Sylvain SONNET/123RF; **p38:** sherly348 / 500px/Getty Images; **p40(a):** World Food Programme; **p40(b):** Save the Children Fund; p40(c): Oxfam Logo/Oxfam GB; **p40(d):** International Federation of Red Cross and Red Crescent Societies; **p40(e):** Médecins Sans Frontières (MSF); **p41:** OsherR/Shutterstock; **p42:** mentalmind/Shutterstock; **p43:** Daniel J. Rao/Shutterstock; p47(l): oriori/Shutterstock; p47(r): JOEL NITO/AFP via Getty Images; **p49:** The History Emporium / Alamy Stock Photo; **p52:** Monkey Business Images/Shutterstock; **p53:** Illustration by Cathy Anholt of Article 22 of the Universal Declaration of Human Rights, from We Are Born Free (Frances Lincoln/Amnesty International 2008); **p54:** TONY KARUMBA/AFP via Getty Images; **p56(l):** Samuel Chunga/World Vision; **p56(r):** Samuel Chunga/World Vision; **p57(t):** Halfpoint/Shutterstock; **p57(b):** DeepakJoshi/Shutterstock; **p58:** Marko Bradic / Shutterstock; **p59:** BEHROUZ MEHRI/AFP via Getty Images; **p60:** Siriwat Nakha/123RF; **p61:** Photoongraphy/Shutterstock; **p63:** JeremyRichards / Shutterstock; **p64(a):** Valentyn Volkov / Shutterstock; **p64(b):** DFabri / Shutterstock; **p64(c):** Sergey Khachatryan / Shutterstock; **p64(d):** Kojiro / Shutterstock; **p67(tl):** © GraphicaArtis / Bridgeman Images; p67(tr): Leo Nicholls; **p67(bl):** Chip Snaddon; **p67(br):** © Adrian Hillman/arcangel; **p68:** Jarek Pawlak/Shutterstock; **p69:** bright/Shutterstock; **p70:** Marco Secchi/Getty Images; **p71:** Bits And Splits/Shutterstock; **p73(t):** DeltaOFF/Shutterstock; **p73(b):** Pat Tuson / Alamy Stock Photo; **p74(tl):** Imagentle/Shutterstock; **p74(tr):** chachastephane/Getty Images; **p74(bl):** anutr tosirikul/Shutterstock; **p74(br):** Võ Lân/Getty Images; **p75:** World History Archive / Alamy Stock Photo; **p76:** Orlok/Shutterstock; **p77:** Contraband Collection / Alamy Stock Photo; **p80(t):** Golden Pixels LLC/Shutterstock; **p80(b):** SpeedKingz/Shutterstock; **p81(t):** Jasmin Merdan/Getty Images; **p81(m):** PhotoTalk/Getty Images; **p81(b):** TONO-BALAGUER/123RF; **p83(t):** PT Images/Shutterstock; **p83(b):** 3000ad/Shutterstock; **p84(t):** Repina Valeriya/Shutterstock; **p84(b):** The Granger Collection / Alamy Stock Photo; **p86:** Simon Bartram; **p89:** Entertainment Pictures / Alamy Stock Photo; **p90:** Frame Stock Footage/Shutterstock; **p91:** Kseniya Ivashkevich/Shutterstock; **p92:** Daria Pozhilova/Shutterstock; **p93:** Gerardo C.Lerner/Shutterstock; **p94:** krasky/Shutterstock; **p95:** sirtravelalot/Shutterstock; **p97(t):** Jonas Petrovas/Shutterstock; **p97(b):** CO Leong/Shutterstock; **p98:** With kind permission of Oregon Shadow Theatre; p99(l): Vladimir Zhoga/Shutterstock; **p99(r):** Justin Creedy Smith / akg-images; **p100:** Tananyaa Pithi/Shutterstock; **p101(t):** Heritage Image Partnership Ltd / Alamy Stock Photo; **p101(b):** Fresh Stock/Shutterstock; **p102:** Album / Alamy Stock Photo; **p103:** Maarten Steunenberg/Shutterstock; **p108:** © Imperial War Museums / Bridgeman Images; **p110(t):** tristan tan/Shutterstock; **p110(b):** Sylvana Rega / Shutterstock; **p111(t):** Darren Whittingham/Shutterstock; **p111(ml):** Martin Fowler/Shutterstock; **p111(mr):** Zoart Studio/Shutterstock; **p111(bl):** ultimathule / Shutterstock; **p111(br):** original images / Alamy Stock Photo; **p112:** Wang LiQiang/Shutterstock; **p113(t):** ultimathule / Shutterstock; **p113(t):** sdamienk/Shutterstock **p113(b):** Wire. Dog / Alamy Stock Photo; **p114:** Malcolm Fairman / Alamy Stock Photo; **p115(t):** Harley Schwadron/Cartoonstock; **p115(b):** Vahan Shirvanian/Cartoonstock; **p116(t):** MasterBliss / Alamy Stock Photo; **p116(b):** ZouZou/Shutterstock; **p117(t):** Riccardo Mayer/Shutterstock; **p117(m):** Scarabea/Shutterstock; **p117(b):** Free Wind 2014/Shutterstock; **p119:** © Brian Adams; **p120:** Design Pics Inc / Alamy Stock Photo; **p122:** vulcano/Shutterstock; **p123:** Preto Perola/Shutterstock; **p124(l):** JinYoung Lee / Shutterstock; **p124(r):** Steve Lagreca / Alamy Stock Photo; **p125:** Ok.nazarenko / Shutterstock; **p126:** Johnathan21/Shutterstock; **p127:** phototr/Shutterstock; **p129:** Pictorial Press Ltd / Alamy Stock Photo; **p130(t):** Aleksandra Madejska/Shutterstock; **p130(b):** Historica Graphica Collection/Heritage Images/Getty Images; **p131:** JJs / Alamy Stock Photo; **p132:** Henk Bogaard/Shutterstock; **p134(l):** agefotostock / Alamy Stock Photo; **p134(r):** The Picture Art Collection / Alamy Stock Photo; **p135:** PAINTING / Alamy Stock Photo; **p136:** GRANGER / Alamy Stock Photo; **p137:** photolibrary.com/Getty Images; **p138:** tororo reaction/Shutterstock; **p140:** History and Art Collection / Alamy Stock Photo; **p142:** Mark Boulton / Alamy Stock Photo; **p143:** Johan Swanepoel/Shutterstock; **p143:** Anup Shah/Getty Images; **p145:** Mark Boulton / Alamy Stock Photo; **p146:** daseaford/Shutterstock; **p147:** Radu Bighian / EyeEm/Getty Images; **p148:** PA Images / Alamy Stock Photo; **p151:** MDV Edwards/Shutterstock; **p153:** Yaroslaff/Shutterstock; **p154:** niloo138/Shutterstock; **p155:** fivespots/Shutterstock; **p156:** Anant Kasetsinsombut/Shutterstock; **p157:** Matthew W Keefe/Shutterstock; **p162:** Brian Kinney/Shutterstock; **p163:** Chronicle / Alamy Stock Photo; **p164:** Ministry of Fisheries via Getty Images; **p166:** Mark Trail © 2006 North America Syndicate, Inc, World Rights Reserved; **p167(tl):** paulwolf/123RF; **p167(tr):** Heidi's Pics/Shutterstock; **p167(bl):** Menno Schaefer/Shutterstock; **p167(br):** BobNoah/Shutterstock; **p168:** Sueddeutsche Zeitung Photo / Alamy Stock Photo; **p170:** danishkhan/Shutterstock; **p172(t):** © Asian Art & Archaeology, Inc./CORBIS/Corbis via Getty Images; **p172(b):** 泉 lin / Alamy Stock Photo; **p173:** Vadim Petrako/Shutterstock; **p174:** North Wind Picture Archives / Alamy Stock Photo; **p176:** History and Art Collection / Alamy Stock Photo; **p178:** Richard Seeley/Shutterstock; **p179(t):** Ivan Cano/Getty Images; **p179(m):** Kiev. Victor/Shutterstock; **p179(b):** Varenyk/Shutterstock; **p180:** debstheleo/Getty Images; **p181:** Peter Macdiarmid/Getty Images; **p182:** Fotopogledi/Shutterstock; **p183(t):** vectorfusionart/Shutterstock; **p183(b):** adwo/Shutterstock; **p184(t):** EpicStockMedia/Shutterstock; **p184(b):** PA Images / Alamy Stock Photo; **p186:** Madlen/Shutterstock; akhnyushchy/Shutterstock; Ase/Shutterstock; nujimomo/iStockphoto; DNY59/iStockphoto; Elenarts/iStockphoto; **p190:** Jenny/WireImage via Getty Images; **p191:** Pedro Guimaraes / Guardian / eyevine; **p192:** Creative Family/Shutterstock.

Artwork by Dan Gartman, Judy Brown, Mark Draisey, and Q2A Media.

Joy Adamson: extract from *Born Free* (Pan Macmillan, 2010), copyright © Joy Adamson 1966, reprinted by permission of the publishers, Pan Macmillan through PLSclear.
John Agard: 'The Windrush Child' from *Half Caste* (Hodder Children's Books, 2004), copyright © John Agard 1998, reprinted by permission of John Agard c/o Caroline Sheldon Literary Agency Ltd
Mallen Baker: 'Ellen MacArthur - Showing how we can thrive on limited resources', from mallenbaker.net, reprinted by permission of the author.
Renato Barros as told to Jennifer Lucy Allan: 'Experience: I founded my own Country', guardian.com, 14 Nov 2014, copyright © Guardian News and Media Ltd 2014, 2022, reprinted by permission of GNM Ltd.
David Calcutt: extract from Act 3, Scene 3 of *Treasure Island* by Robert Louis Stevenson (Oxford Playscripts, 2017), script copyright © David Calcutt 2012, reprinted by permission of Oxford Publishing Ltd through PLSclear.
Frank Cottrell Boyce: 'Leader of Men', book review of *Nation* by Terry Pratchett, guardian.com, 13 Sept 2008, copyright © Guardian News and Media Ltd 2008, 2022, reprinted by permission of GNM Ltd.
Anita Desai: abridged extract from *The Village by the Sea: An Indian Family Story* (Puffin, 1984), copyright © Anita Desai 1984, reprinted by permission of Penguin Books Ltd and the author c/o Rogers, Coleridge & White Ltd, 20 Powis Mews, London W11 1JN.
Nissim Ezekiel: 'Touching' from *The Latter-day Psalms* (OUP India, 1982), reprinted by permission of Oxford University Press, India.
Robert Frost: 'The Road Not Taken' from *The Poetry of Robert Frost* edited by Edward Connery Lathem (Jonathan Cape, 1971), copyright © 1916, 1969 by Henry Holt & Company, copyright © 1944 by Robert Frost, reproduced by permission of The Random House Group Ltd, Penguin Random House UK, and Henry Holt & Company. All rights reserved.
Romesh Gunesekera: extract from 'Kolla' in *Reef* (Penguin, 1994), copyright © Romesh Gunesekera 1994, reprinted by permission of Granta Books and The New Press, www.thenewpress.com.
Shusha Guppy: extract from *The Blindfold Horse* (Penguin, 1989), copyright © The Estate of Shusha Guppy 1988, reprinted by permission of Aitken Alexander Associates.
Minfong Ho: extract from 'What a Wonderful Thing' in *The Clay Marble* (Farrar, Straus & Giroux, 1991), copyright © Minfong Ho 1991, reprinted by permission of Farrar, Straus & Giroux, and the author, c/o McIntosh & Otis, Inc. All rights reserved.
Ghada Karmi: extract from *In Search of Fatima: A Palestinian Story* (2e, Verso, 2009), copyright © Ghada Karmi 2002, reprinted by permission of Verso through PLSclear.
Elizabeth Lutzeier: extract from *The Coldest Winter* (OUP, 2002), copyright © Elizabeth Lutzeier 2002, reprinted by permission of Oxford Publishing Ltd through PLSclear.
Walter de la Mare: extract from 'The Listeners' from *The Complete Poems of Walter de la Mare* (Faber, 1973), reprinted by permission of The Literary Trustees of Walter de la Mare and the Society of Authors as their Representative.
Kathy Marks: extract from 'Monsters from the Deep', *The Independent*, 23.2.2007, copyright © Kathy Marks/The Independent 2007, reprinted by permission of ESI Media Syndication/Independent News & Media Ltd.
Geraldine McCaughrean: extract from retelling of *Moby Dick or the White Whale* by Herman Melville (OUP, 2016), copyright © Geraldine McCaughrean 1996, reprinted by permission of Davi Higham Associates.
Ved Mehta: extract from *Vedi* (OUP Inc, 1982), first published in *The New Yorker*, reprinted by permission of Oxford Publishing Ltd, through PLSclear.
Thomas Merton: 'The Joy of Fishes' by Chuang Tzu translated by Thomas Merton from *The Way of Chuang Tzu* (New Directions, 1965), copyright © 1965 by The Abbey of Gethsemani, reprinted by permission of New Directions Publishing Corp.
Kiran Millwood Hargrave: extracts from *The Island At the End of Everything* (Chicken House, 2017), copyright © Kiran Millwood Hargrave 2017, reprinted by permission of Chicken House Ltd. All right reserved.
Grace Nichols: 'Island Man' from *The Fat Black Woman's Poems* (Virago, 2003), copyright © Grace Nichols 1984, reprinted by permission of the publishers, Little, Brown Book Group Ltd through PLSclear.
Mira Stout: extract from *One Thousand Chestnut Trees* (Flamingo, 1997), copyright © Mira Stout 1997, reprinted by permission of the author and HarperCollins Publishers Ltd.
G P Taylor: extract from *Shadowmancer* (Faber, 2003), copyright © G P Taylor 2002, reprinted by permission of Faber & Faber Ltd, and G P Taylor c/o Markosia Enterprises Ltd.
UN News: 'Madagascar: Severe drought could spur world's first climate change famine', *UN News*, 21 Oct 2021, https://news.un.org/en/story/2021/10/1103712, used with permission.
Rachel Redford: dramatized extract from *Great Expectations* by Charles Dickens; retelling of traditional tales, 'A Drop of Honey' (from Myanmar) and 'Androcles and the Lion' (Aesop); 'The disappearing village'; and translation of 'Don't Believe in War' by Bulat Okudzhava; all written for the first edition and reused by permission of the author.

Any third party use of this material outside this publication, is prohibited. Interested parties should apply to the copyright holders indicated in each case.

Although we have made every effort to trace and contact all copyright holders before publication this has not been possible in all cases. If notified, the publisher will rectify any errors or omissions at the earliest opportunity.

The manufacturer's authorised representative in the EU for product safety is Oxford University Press España S.A. of El Parque Empresarial San Fernando de Henares, Avenida de Castilla, 2 – 28830 Madrid (www.oup.es/en or product.safety@oup.com).
OUP España S.A. also acts as importer into Spain of products made by the manufacturer.

Contents

How do we cross rivers?

> **'Let's build bridges, not walls'**
> Martin Luther King, Jr.

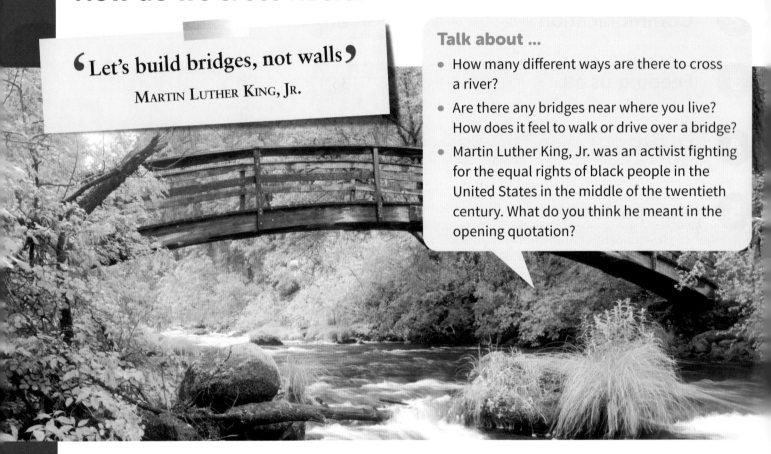

Talk about ...

- How many different ways are there to cross a river?
- Are there any bridges near where you live? How does it feel to walk or drive over a bridge?
- Martin Luther King, Jr. was an activist fighting for the equal rights of black people in the United States in the middle of the twentieth century. What do you think he meant in the opening quotation?

A bridge is a physical structure which allows us to cross over an obstacle, for example a river, a road, or a valley. Bridges can be a powerful symbol, often representing communication, connection, teamwork and progress.

Many popular idioms refer to bridges. What do you think the following mean?

- To burn one's bridges
- To be water under the bridge
- To cross that bridge later
- A bridge too far
- To bridge the gap

How do we build bridges?

Building bridges requires ingenuity. Over the centuries, there have been many innovations in bridge-building techniques. In this unit, you will learn about some of them.

Bridge building has historically been important to the growth of towns and cities, as well as to enable people to cross rivers, mountains and valleys. The Romans built bridges to help expand their empire across Europe.

Roman bridges are often supported by circular stone arches, which allows a bridge to cover a larger area than the older style of stone slab or wooden beam bridges. An amazing example of a Roman bridge built using arches is the Pont du Gard aqueduct, which was built in 14 CE.

The Pont du Gard aqueduct near Nîmes, southern France

How many different kinds of bridges are there?

Try to name all the different kinds of bridges you can think of in small groups. These days, most bridges make use of one or more of the five basic bridge types: the beam, the arch, the truss, the suspension and the cable-stayed bridge. In each case, the bridge builders need to know what the bridge will be used for (for example, for road, rail or pedestrian use, or all combined) in order to decide on the best methods and materials for its construction.

- Work out the meaning of new words
- Look at where words come from

Word origins

ingenuity (n), meaning 'cleverness in making or inventing things'; comes from the Latin word *ingenium*, meaning 'natural talent'
Related word:
• ingenious

aqueduct (n), comes from two Latin words, *aqua*, meaning 'water', and *ducere*, meaning 'to lead'

Glossary

innovation new method, idea, product

expand become or make larger or more extensive

empire large group of states or countries ruled over by a single monarch, group or sovereign state

arches curved symmetrical structures spanning openings

slab large, thick, flat piece of stone or concrete

beam long, strong piece of timber or metal used to support the roof or floor of a structure

Learning tip
Try to use new words when you write or talk about a topic. Look for connections – maybe you can remember opposites or word roots. Make a list of related technical terms.

Types of bridge construction

Beam bridge

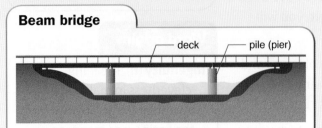

This type of bridge is a good design when trying to span a short gap that is also not very high. A **beam bridge** is supported at each end by land or tall columns. (A column is also called a pier or a pile.)

Arch bridge 1

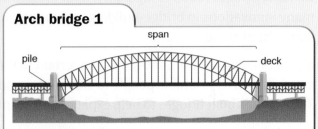

An **arch bridge** supports weight because it is squeezed together. This squeezing force is carried along the curve to the supports at each end. Building an arch bridge is difficult because it is completely unstable until it meets in the middle.

Arch bridge 2

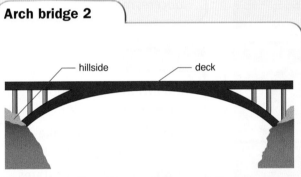

This is another form of the **arch bridge** used in valley or hillside locations to bridge land masses. Some of the most spectacular bridges have been built in remote mountain locations using this difficult and adaptable form of construction.

Suspension bridge

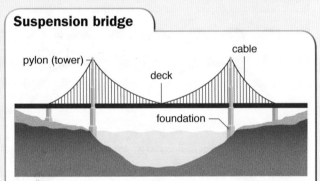

The **suspension bridge** is the best kind of bridge to go over a large body of water. A suspension bridge hangs from steel cables. Because the deck is hung in the air, it must be either heavy or stiff, or both, to limit movement.

Truss bridge

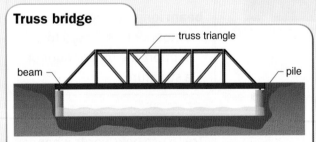

The **truss bridge** is like a beam bridge except that it is much stronger. These bridges use a truss pattern of triangles for structural support. Truss bridges are often used for railway bridges as they can support the great weight and vibrations of the trains.

Cable-stayed bridge

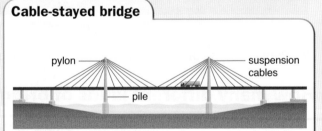

A **cable-stayed bridge** is like a suspension bridge, but the cables are tied directly from the deck to the pylon towers instead of from a hanging cable. Cable-stayed bridges use less cable and can be built much faster than suspension bridges.

Another famous bridge

Below is a text about an ancient wooden bridge in the university city of Cambridge, UK.

The Mathematical Bridge

The city of Cambridge boasts as many as 24 bridges. They cross the River Cam which gives the city its name. One of the most recognizable of these bridges is the Mathematical Bridge – also known simply as the Wooden Bridge – which connects
5 two buildings of Queens' College (Cambridge University) on either side of the River Cam.

Local legend has it that Sir Isaac Newton was the mastermind behind the bridge's design. Newton, the man who introduced the world to the law of gravity, was a Fellow and Professor of
10 Mathematics at Trinity College (Cambridge University). The story goes that Newton designed the bridge so it could be constructed without any fixings (nut and bolts) at the joints. The legend describes a group of students who took the bridge apart to see how it was constructed but then found that they were
15 unable to reconstruct it without using bolts to hold it together.

In truth, the bridge was built in 1749 by James Essex the Younger, 22 years after the death of Isaac Newton. It is true that it has been rebuilt to the same design, but there have always been fixings at the joints. However, the fixings on the
20 original bridge were less visible than those on the current structure, possibly leading to the story of the hapless students. It was rebuilt once in 1866 and again in 1905. In 1866, the bridge deck was changed from
25 a stepped design to the current sloped deck. In 1905, a complete rebuild of the bridge was required due to weathering of the original oak structure.

Glossary

deck road of a bridge
pile vertical support driven into the ground that carries the weight of the bridge
span section between two pylons
pylon tower-like vertical support
suspension cable braided wire that supports a bridge

Talk about ...

Why do you think local people prefer to think of the bridge designer as Isaac Newton? Write down your thoughts.

Comprehension

- Use implicit and explicit evidence from a text to answer questions
- Explain how punctuation creates effects
- Discuss a topic using specialized vocabulary

A

Look at 'Types of bridge construction'.

1 Which is the best construction to use to bridge a valley between two mountains?

2 What is another word for a column?

3 Which construction is mostly used on railway lines? Why?

4 Which type of bridge would you choose to span a wide river?

5 What advantage does a cable-stayed bridge have over a suspension bridge?

B

Look at 'The Mathematical Bridge'.

1 Give one word in the first paragraph that shows that local people are proud of Cambridge's bridges.

2 Explain why dashes are used in the first paragraph.

3 Give two phrases in the second paragraph that suggest that the legend about Isaac Newton and the building of the bridge isn't true.

4 Give one word in the third paragraph which means the same as the word 'unfortunate'.

Can you solve this puzzle?

Ali, John, Haniya and Maria are on holiday in Sri Lanka. They are out walking when they come to an old wooden bridge suspended over a wild river. The bridge is weak and only able to carry the weight of two of them at a time. They need to get over the bridge as quickly as possible as it is getting dark. To keep safe, they need a torch for each crossing. However, they only have one torch between them and the bridge is too long to throw the torch back across the bridge.

John has hurt his leg and is limping so it will take him 10 minutes to cross the bridge. Haniya has blisters on her feet so it will take her 5 minutes to walk across slowly. Maria can walk across quickly in 2 minutes and Ali can jog across in 1 minute.

Ali thinks for a moment and declares that the crossing can be completed in 17 minutes. There is no trick. How is it done?

Be a bridge builder

In small groups, use paper to construct your own type of bridge between two books of equal thickness. Have a competition to see which group can design the bridge that carries the most weight. You can test how strong and sturdy the bridge is by using coins or small stones.

Stretch zone

Look at the photo of the stone bridge. Write one paragraph explaining why the arch does not collapse.

Present your favourite bridge

Find pictures of famous bridges around the world. Use the text 'Types of bridge construction' on page 6 to work out which type of construction each bridge uses. Can you find a picture of each type of bridge construction?

Choose one of the bridges to research. You are going to make notes for a presentation. Find out about its:

- geographical position (Where in the world is it? What areas does it connect?)
- history (When was it built? Has it been rebuilt at any time?)
- structure (What makes it strong? How is the weight distributed?)
- importance (Why is it famous? Is it an important landmark? How does it benefit local people?)
- significance to the history of bridge design and construction.

Make an illustration or a 3D model to explain the technical features of your bridge. Use your notes and visual support material to make a presentation in class.

- Research a topic from different sources and make notes
- Make a presentation, using verbal and non-verbal techniques

Students in Budapest, Hungary add more weight to their pasta bridge. How much more before it breaks?

Rialto Bridge, Venice, Italy

9

- Contribute to group discussion and communicate ideas confidently
- Discuss a topic using specialized vocabulary

Can you identify these bridges?

Match the photos to the notes below.

The Chengyang Bridge over the Linxi River in China's Guangxi province has a covered corridor and five pagoda-style pavilions erected over the piers. Covered bridges, traditional to this region, are also known as 'wind-and-rain' bridges.

The Garabit Viaduct spans the Truyère River near Ruynes-en-Margeride, Cantal, France. The bridge was constructed between 1880 and 1884 by Gustave Eiffel before he began work on the Eiffel Tower.

Isambard Kingdom Brunel won a competition in 1830 for his design of the Clifton Suspension Bridge over the River Avon in Bristol, UK. At the time of construction (completed 1864), it had the longest span of any bridge in the world.

The Stari Most (meaning 'old bridge' in English) crosses the River Neretva in Mostar, Bosnia Herzegovina. The bridge was commissioned by Suleiman the Magnificent in 1557 to replace an older wooden bridge. It was destroyed in 1993 in the Bosnian War and rebuilt in 1997.

This bridge was made famous by the film and the novel, *The Bridge over the River Kwai*, based on the experience of POWs who worked on the Thailand–Burma railway in the 1940s.

The Tarr Steps in Somerset, UK, is an old stone clapper bridge, made without any cement or mortar. Historians are divided over it possibly dating back to pre-historic times and it (more likely) having medieval origins of circa 1400 CE.

Built in 1973, the Bosphorus Bridge in Turkey links the two sides of Istanbul and the continents of Asia and Europe.

This suspended rope bridge over the lagoon at Sentosa, Singapore, is only for pedestrians. It swings and sways as you walk.

A Land Rover is crossing a log bridge, which could be anywhere in the world.

- Work out the meaning of new words
- Discuss a topic using specialized vocabulary

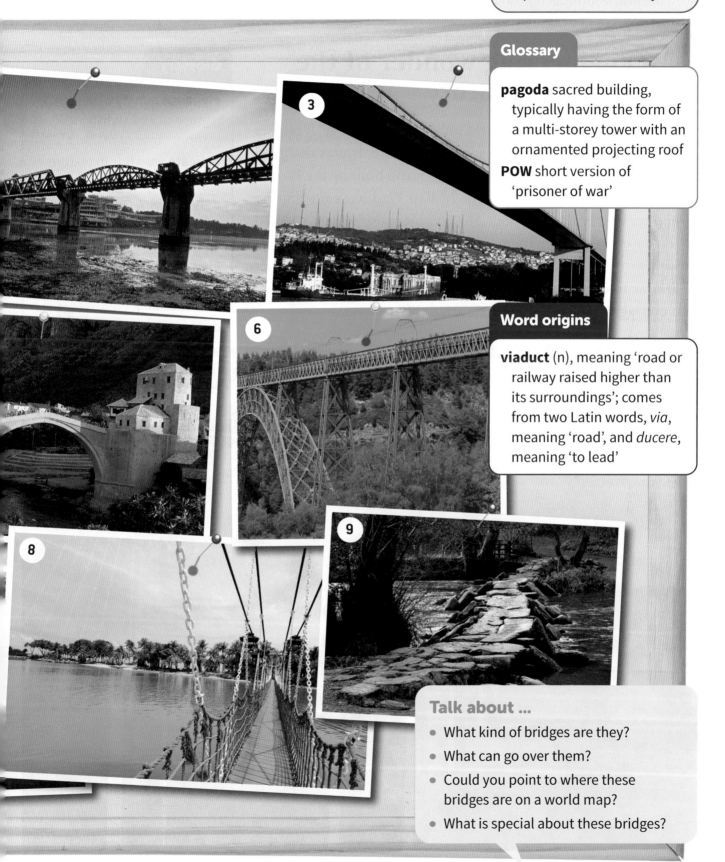

Glossary

pagoda sacred building, typically having the form of a multi-storey tower with an ornamented projecting roof

POW short version of 'prisoner of war'

Word origins

viaduct (n), meaning 'road or railway raised higher than its surroundings'; comes from two Latin words, *via*, meaning 'road', and *ducere*, meaning 'to lead'

Talk about ...

- What kind of bridges are they?
- What can go over them?
- Could you point to where these bridges are on a world map?
- What is special about these bridges?

- Recognize the structure and main features of a newspaper article

Spotlight: Millau Viaduct, France

Read the article introduction and fact file on the Millau Viaduct.

An engineering wonder of the twenty-first century

The Millau Viaduct is the world's highest road bridge. It crosses the River Tarn at Millau in southern France. It was designed by the British architect Norman Foster and built by the French construction group Eiffage. The Millau Viaduct is the highest
5 and heaviest bridge ever built. However, it is also widely admired for its elegance, apparent lightness and delicate structure as well as its sheer strength. Not only does the Millau Viaduct appear to defy gravity, but it is also a magnificent example of a courageous work of modern art.

Glossary

elegance quality of being graceful and stylish in appearance or manner

delicate very fine in texture or structure

defy disobey, resist or not follow the normal order of things

elevated situated or placed higher than the surrounding area

dual carriageway road with two or more lanes in each direction

road toll payment that drivers must pay to use a road

The Millau Viaduct, built in Southern Massif Central, France

- Recognize the structure and main features of a fact file
- Write a fact file

FACT FILE

- Millau is pronounced 'me-yo'.
- Construction was completed in 2004.
- Height: 343 metres at its highest point, making it the most elevated roadway in the world. It is higher than the Eiffel Tower.
- Total length: 2.4 kilometres.
- Width: 25 metres. The dual carriageway is suspended nearly 250 metres above the River Tarn. The deck structure is light but very strong.
- Weight: 242,000 tonnes (36,000 of steel and 206,000 of concrete).
- The Millau Viaduct will carry 10,000 vehicles a day, rising to 25,000 during the summer.
- It took more than 500 people three years to construct the bridge.
- The £276 million cost will be repaid by road tolls.
- The road slopes down at a 30° angle from north to south.

Comprehension

 A

1 What kind of bridge is the Millau Viaduct?
2 What was the final cost of building the bridge?
3 How is France able to pay for the building of the bridge?

 B

1 The bridge is admired for its 'delicate structure' and 'lightness'. Explain in your own words how this can be the case when the bridge is also heavier than any other bridge in the world.

2 What are the writer's own opinions of the bridge? Give two opinions.

3 The Millau Viaduct is the highest bridge in the world. 'Highest' is a superlative. The superlative is formed by the suffix -est (for example, 'smallest') or by the word 'most' before the adjective (for example, 'most beautiful'). Find another example of each kind of superlative form in the article or fact file.

4 Write down more superlative forms (for example, 'the most beautiful', 'the most dangerous', 'the longest', 'the oldest').

 C

1 The article introduction describes the creation of the bridge as 'courageous'. Do you agree? Why? Why not?

Language tip

Adjectives and adverbs come in three different forms: the positive (such as 'high', 'comfortable'), the comparative (such as 'higher', 'more comfortable') and the superlative (such as 'highest', 'most comfortable').

Comparative: used to compare one person, thing, action or state to another.

For example: 'This bridge is higher than the Eiffel Tower.'

Superlative: used to compare one thing to all others in the same category.

For example: 'This bridge is the highest bridge in France.'

 Stretch zone

Write down the superlative forms of 'much', 'bad', 'little' and 'far'.

Write your own fact file

Choose a famous bridge from another country and write a fact file about it.

- Read and enjoy autobiography set in a different time and culture
- Recognize the structure and main features of autobiography
- Work out the meaning of new words

A frightening experience

The events in the following text took place in Russia over 200 years ago. Ivan was in charge of the family servants who were bringing the writer, Sergei Askanoff, home from school for the summer holidays. They had to cross the River Kama by ferryboat. At the time, Sergei was just nine years old.

Crossing the river

In the afternoon we reached the bank of the Kama River. Opposite us was the village to which we were going to cross by ferryboat. On the bank, waiting to cross with us, were three loaded carts with their drivers, and a group of villagers. The
5 women were carrying baskets full of berries which they were carrying home. The ferryboat was tied to the bank, but there was no ferryman to row us across the river. After some discussion, the villagers and my family servants decided to take us across the river themselves. One of the villagers said he had been a
10 ferryman for some years so he would take the steering oar and guide the ferryboat across.

The mighty Kama, one of Russia's major rivers

- Read and enjoy autobiography set in a different time and culture
- Recognize the structure and main features of autobiography
- Work out the meaning of new words

15 The ferryboat was loaded. The three carts with their drivers, my carriage with its three horses and my family servants, the villagers and the women with their baskets were all loaded on board. The man who said he was a ferryman took his place at the steering oar. My servant Ivan had the courage and strength of ten men and he and some villagers took the other oars.

Although the village was directly opposite, we had to row upstream for more than a verst before turning across the river. 20 This was to avoid the current of the angry Kama River.

The boat was moving slowly upstream when a black cloud suddenly appeared and covered the horizon. A violent summer storm was approaching. To save time, the men rowed only part of the necessary verst upstream. They then murmured a prayer 25 and started to row straight across the river. But before we reached the middle of the river, the sky and the water grew black, the wind blew like a hurricane, and thunder and lightning broke over us. The man at the steering oar dropped his oar in panic and confessed that he had never been a ferryman and 30 could not steer. The women shrieked in terror. I was so frightened that I just shook with terror and could not make a sound.

The current carried us down several versts to a sandbank in the river about a hundred yards from the bank, where we came to a halt. Ivan sprang into the chest-high water. He made the 35 quietest of our horses jump off the ferryboat. He managed to put me on it and told me to hang onto the horse's mane. Then he led the horse by its bridle as great waves of black water rushed past. Suddenly Ivan disappeared into deep water and my horse began to swim. I have never forgotten the terror 40 which I felt at that moment.

I felt as though I was drowning in the great black waves, but Ivan was a strong swimmer. He swam on to the shallow water where he could stand without letting go of the horse's bridle. Then he brought us safely to the bank. I was taken off the 45 horse almost unconscious with my hands stiff from clinging to the horse's mane. Soon I recovered and was very happy to find that everyone was safe.

SERGEI ASKANOFF

Glossary

ferryboat boat or ship for conveying passengers and goods, especially as a regular service over a short distance

steering oar oversized oar or board to control the direction of a ship before the invention of the rudder

verst old Russian measurement of distance – about one kilometre

current water moving downhill in a river

hurricane storm with a violent wind, in particular a tropical cyclone in the Caribbean

bridle headgear used to control a horse

- Discuss the context and setting in which a story is written
- Explore how setting and character are developed
- Use context in a text to identify word class
- Write an account, using a model text

Comprehension

1 What kind of boat took the people across the river? How was it powered?
2 What had the women been doing?
3 Why did the ferryboat have to go upstream before crossing the river?
4 What do you think a sandbank is? (line 32)
5 What's the difference between chest-high water, deep water and shallow water?

1 Look at the following words from the text. Use the context in the text to decide whether the word is a verb or a noun. Then match each word to its correct definition.

Word	Meaning
bank (line 1)	come to a sudden stop
murmured (line 24)	growth of long hair on the neck of a horse, lion or other mammal
confessed (line 29)	the land alongside or sloping down to a river or lake
halt (line 34)	said something in a low voice
mane (line 36)	admitted committing a crime or doing something wrong

2 How does the author build up the tension and sense of fear in the fourth paragraph?
3 Why do you think one of the villagers lied about his previous experience on ferryboats?
4 What sort of man do you think Ivan is?

1 Think about frightening experiences you have had. Take turns to describe your frightening experience. What happened? How did you resolve the situation? What could you have done to stop the situation from happening or to make the situation better? Whose was the most frightening experience?

Write about your experiences

Choose one of the frightening experiences and write an account. Remember to include lots of exciting adverbs and adjectives as well as powerful verbs.

 Stretch zone

An autobiography is what a writer writes about his or her own life. The ancient Greek word *auto* means 'self'. Can you think of some other words which begin with the prefix *auto*-? For example, the first cars were called 'automobiles' because they moved by themselves without horses pulling them.

- Explain how language features and figurative language create effects

When do bridges and rivers mean something else?

Look back at the idioms on page 4. Sometimes when writers use the phrases 'building bridges' or 'crossing rivers', they mean something else. You are not meant to take the meaning literally but metaphorically.

Writers, poets and artists often build bridges in their minds, and use the image as a metaphor, a poetic idea, or a way of talking about things differently.

We may use an image of crossing a flooded river to talk about another kind of challenge altogether. This challenge may be just as daunting as a big river. Sometimes these metaphors are such good ways to talk about real life that they become idioms and proverbs.

Explaining proverbs

What is a proverb? How are proverbs different to idioms? What do you think each of these three proverbs means? (Sometimes we know their sources, sometimes we don't!)

It's a big river indeed that cannot be crossed.
(Maori proverb from New Zealand)

Don't change horses while crossing a river.

If you are good at building bridges, you will never fall into the abyss!

Think of a situation that would fit each proverb.
- Consider how you will explain the situation to your classmates.
- Include a lot of detail on the circumstances and background.
- Describe the feelings of those involved.

Walls or bridges?

What did Martin Luther King, Jr. mean when he said, "Let's build bridges, not walls"?

At his inauguration as South African leader in 1994, Nelson Mandela said: "The time for the healing of the wounds has come. The moment to bridge the chasms that divide us has come. The time to build is upon us." What idea do you think he was trying to express? What do you think 'the chasms that divide us' are and what metaphorical bridges could be built to bring us together?

Stretch zone

Think of more proverbs and idioms connected to bridges or crossing rivers. Explain what they mean.

Word origins

literally (adv), refers to a straight interpretation of the facts; comes from the Latin word *littera*, meaning 'letter of the alphabet'
Related words:
- literal
- literature
- letter

metaphorically (adv), refers to saying one thing to mean another; comes via Latin from the Greek verb *metapherein*, meaning 'to transfer'
Related words:
- metaphor
- metaphorical

Glossary

inauguration formal ceremony to establish a new leader
chasm deep opening in the ground

Nelson Mandela

Building bridges

See if you can work out the writer's message in this poem.

The Bridge Builder

An old man, going a lone highway,
Came, at the evening, cold and gray,
To a chasm, vast, and deep, and wide,
Through which was flowing a sullen tide.
5 The old man crossed in the twilight dim;
The sullen stream had no fears for him;
But he turned, when safe on the other side,
And built a bridge to span the tide.

"Old man," said a fellow pilgrim, near,
10 "You are wasting strength with building here;
Your journey will end with the ending day;
You never again must pass this way;
You have crossed the chasm, deep and wide,
Why build you the bridge at the eventide?"

15 The builder lifted his old gray head:
"Good friend, in the path I have come," he said,
"There followeth after me today
A youth, whose feet must pass this way.
This chasm, that has been naught to me,
20 To that fair-haired youth may a pitfall be.
He, too, must cross in the twilight dim;
Good friend, I am building the bridge for him."

WILL ALLEN DROMGOOLE

Glossary

highway main road
sullen bad-tempered and sulky
tide alternate rising and falling of the sea
twilight soft glowing light from the sky when the sun is going down below the horizon
pilgrim person who travels a long distance to visit a significant place
eventide end of the day; evening

- Use implicit and explicit evidence from a text to answer questions
- Explain how structure and language features create effects
- Write an article

Comprehension

A

1 What problem does the old man face?
2 Why is his fellow pilgrim surprised by the old man's actions?
3 What explanation does the old man give for building the bridge?
4 Who does the third pilgrim represent?
5 Copy and complete the table below by writing **three** adjectives to describe each of the pilgrims' characters.

> experienced practical curious inexperienced helpful carefree innocent self-centred considerate

The old pilgrim	The fellow pilgrim	The young pilgrim

B

1 What is the rhyme scheme of the poem? What kind of feeling does this create?
2 Give an example of personification from the first stanza.
3 Look at the following phrases. What do they mean?
- 'span the tide' (line 8)
- 'never again must pass this way' (line 12)
- 'naught to me' (line 19)

C

1 In pairs, discuss the main themes of the poem and what message the poem is conveying.
2 Did you enjoy the poem? What did you like/dislike most about the poem?
3 What kind of things can this generation do to help the next generation or make the next generation's life better?

?

Look back at 'The Bridge Builder'. What chasms can you imagine in your own life? Who would you behave like – the pilgrim who found a way across and moved on, or the old man who found a way across and then built a bridge to make the way easier for others? Explain your choice.

Write a magazine article

Imagine that you face a great challenge in your life – one you are not sure you can overcome. Someone like the old pilgrim arrives. They help you to face up to the challenge and conquer it. Write an article for your school magazine about the experience and how it affected your life. Think about:

- the challenge you faced
- who the old pilgrim was (for example, a friend, teacher, or family member)
- how they helped you overcome the challenge and how that made you feel.

② Communication

How do we communicate without words?

> ❝The most important thing in communication is hearing what isn't said❞
>
> PETER DRUCKER

Talk about ...

- What does the quotation mean? Do you think that this is always true?
- Friendships and relationships often break down due to poor communication between people. Do you think it is important that friends can communicate well with each other? Why? Why not?
- What is the best way to communicate with someone? What skills characterize a good listener?
- Apart from the words spoken, how else is a message communicated?

When we think about communication, we usually think about speech, reading and writing, email, texting, and so on. All these methods of communication use words, whether written or spoken.

Communication without words is called 'non-verbal'. The most basic form of non-verbal communication is the expression on our faces. We also express our emotions through:

- our body language – think about what happens to your shoulders when you are sad
- our hands – what happens to your hands when you are excited?

Often it is not what we say, but how we say it that matters most.

Word origins

verbal (adj), comes from the Latin word *verbum*, meaning 'word'
Related word:
  • verbalize

mime (n), comes from the Greek word *mimos*, meaning 'mimic'

- Read non-fiction
- Recognize the structure and main features of a magazine article
- Work out the meaning of new words

Lost for words

Have you heard the saying 'lost for words'? The great French mime artist Marcel Marceau suggested that words cannot express our deepest, most moving emotions. Such feelings are too intense to explain or describe in words. Do you agree? How else might these emotions be expressed?

This article provides some background to the history of the art of mime and the character of the Pierrot. Marcel Marceau liked to dress up as Pierrot when he was performing.

Beyond words

The greatest mime artist of modern times was Marcel Marceau. In the 1950s when he was at the height of his career, he gave 300 performances worldwide each year. With his red flower and his white painted face, Marceau was understood all over
5 the world. "Mime, like music, has neither borders nor nationalities," he explained. In fact, the Master of Silence, as he was known, spoke five languages fluently and was extremely talkative offstage. His performances, however, were wordless.

At the age of five, in 1928, Marceau saw the great comedian
10 Charlie Chaplin in a silent film. Immediately Marceau began to imitate people, birds and even plants! In silent films the actors did not speak, but short written summaries of what was happening appeared on the screen for the audience to read. Marceau's challenge was to fire the audience's imagination
15 without any words at all. Through the movements of his body he expressed everything – from beauty, comedy and conflict to despair, tragedy and hope.

Mime has a long history. In ancient Greece, it was a form of theatre where scenes from everyday life taught moral lessons.
20 In the Theatre of Dionysus in Athens, masked actors performed outdoors to audiences of thousands. When the Romans conquered Greece, they brought the Greek art of mime back to Italy. Under Emperor Augustus of Rome, mime was very popular. This continued into the Middle Ages in Europe with morality plays.

Marcel Marceau miming a story on stage

Glossary

conflict serious disagreement or argument
despair complete loss of hope
morality plays which portray a lesson about good behaviour and character, popular in the fifteenth and early sixteenth centuries

- Read non-fiction
- Recognize the structure and main features of a magazine article
- Work out the meaning of new words

25   In sixteenth-century Italy, touring groups of comic actors known as the *commedia dell' arte* entertained people with their comedy routines and their invention of a set of stock characters that were easy to identify by their masks, costumes and names. One such character is the Harlequin, who was an acrobat and a clown.

30   The traditional Harlequin character was introduced to France in the 1570s. In France, the Harlequin character became known as the Pierrot. The Pierrot is a clown and a sad loner who never found what he was looking

35   for in life. In the 1940s, Marcel Marceau created his character Bip in the tradition of Pierrot. He too was a melancholy man who never realized his dreams.

The art of silence is very much alive today.

40   There are mime theatres all over the world. One of Marceau's famous performances was 'Walking Against the Wind' in which he mimed walking into a strong wind. The singer Michael Jackson borrowed his famous

45   'moonwalk' from this performance, which many dancers have copied since. Mime artists can be seen entertaining people on many city streets today. Some earn money by making themselves into white statues

50   that make intermittent movements to alarm, delight and intrigue passers-by.

Pierrot and Harlequin by
Paul Cézanne, painted in 1888

Talk about ...
- How would you summarize Marceau's views on communication?
- Which emotions, or what Marceau calls 'moving moments', do you think would be difficult to express in words?
- Can you think of a situation in which you were 'lost for words'?

Language tip
Abstract noun: the name for a feeling, idea or concept that you cannot touch.

Examples: 'beauty', 'comedy', 'happiness', 'silence'.

Adjective: a word that describes a noun.

Examples: 'beautiful', 'comic', 'happy', 'silent'.

Glossary

comedy routines short sequences of jokes or humorous actions

stock character stereotypical fictional person or type of person in a work of art

mask covering for all or part of the face, worn as a disguise

acrobat entertainer who performs spectacular gymnastic acts

Comprehension

1 What did Marceau mean when he said mime has "neither borders nor nationalities"? (line 5)

2 What was the difference between Marceau's performances and the silent movies?

3 Give one example which illustrates the fact that mime goes back a long way in the past.

4 Explain the purpose of a mask when used in mime.

1 Write down the meaning of the following words and phrases:
- 'height of his career' (line 2)
- 'offstage' (line 8)
- 'fire the audience's imagination' (line 14)
- 'never realized his dreams' (line 38)
- 'very much alive today' (line 39).

2 Find the words in the text which mean the same as the following:
- to mimic (line 11)
- sad (line 37)
- every now and then (line 50).

3 Explain why the phrase 'in fact' (line 6) is used. What information does it emphasize?

4 Why does the writer use an exclamation mark after 'birds and even plants!'? (line 11)

5 Read through the article again and write down briefly what you think are the key points in each paragraph. Using your notes:
- write a heading for each paragraph
- write a brief summary underneath your heading.

1 Pierrot is a character who first became popular in the late seventeenth century. The image of Pierrot is still popular in art, poetry and plays across many parts of the world. Why do you think the image of Pierrot is so popular in so many different countries?

- Recognize the structure and features of a magazine article
- Use implicit and explicit evidence from the text to answer questions
- Understand the development of ideas and themes in a text
- Use mime to convey a message

Stretch zone

Look at the picture of Marceau on page 21 and Cézanne's painting of Pierrot (in white) on page 22. How did Marceau model himself on the traditional Pierrot? What changes did he make to modernize the character? Why do you think he modelled himself on Pierrot in the first place?

Be a mime artist

Sometimes you have to resort to mime to make yourself understood in a country where you do not speak the language. With a partner, take turns to mime one of the following situations:

- You have been sick all night and have a really bad stomach ache. You go to a pharmacist to buy some medication. Your partner is the pharmacist.
- You are in the middle of a town and want to know the way to the beach. Your partner is the person you ask for directions.

What makes you laugh?

Like mime, pictures in the form of cartoons can make us laugh. They speak to us through visual images, sometimes with the help of a title or caption.

Explain what is going on in the cartoons on this page. Why do we think they are funny?

The latest in communication technology

Voice-activated
High-speed
Wireless
Communications

A dream come true

"It's like I'm actually walking."

- Understand how a point of view can be conveyed in different texts
- Understand the features of a cartoon

Talk about ...

Have you got a favourite cartoon or cartoon character? Why does it make you laugh?

Word origins

caption (n), from the Latin word *capere*, meaning 'to take or seize'
Related words:
- capture
- captive
- encapsulate

cartoon (n), from the Latin word *carta*, our modern use comes via the French word *carton* and Italian word *cartone*, referring to the heavy paper or pasteboard which artists used to draw out their designs

Learning tip

Irony is when something is very different to what is expected. Irony is often funny. What is ironic about these two cartoons? Why do you think irony works well in a cartoon?

Cartoons with purpose

Visual images can also draw attention to serious concerns. Do you think cartoons are an effective way of communicating important, powerful messages?

- Understand how a point of view can be conveyed in different texts
- Understand the features of a cartoon
- Use pictures to communicate personal ideas

?

Can artists, writers and musicians make meaningful change in the world by communicating their concerns through their works of art?

- What is the message being communicated here?
- Why has the artist used an hourglass in the cartoon?
- What is the polar bear's problem?
- What is the man's problem?

Use an image to convey a message

The editor of your local newspaper runs a feature called 'Getting the message across'. Readers are invited to send in a visual image to be included in the feature. Think about something you feel strongly about. It could be something personal, such as keeping siblings out of your bedroom, something national, such as keeping your country's beaches clean, or something global, such as saving an animal from extinction.

First think about the message you want to convey, then decide what image(s) you can use to communicate your message.

 Stretch zone

The hourglass used in this cartoon is a very effective visual symbol. What else could you draw in the top section and in the bottom section? Sketch your own version of the hourglass with different scenes and see if and how the message changes.

What other ways are there to communicate?

How difficult would it be to go to school, make friends or learn the basic skills in life if you could not hear or see? How would you communicate?

American Helen Keller was just 19 months old when she became deaf and blind following an illness. As a child, she was also unable to speak. As Helen grew older, she became wild and uncontrollable because of her extreme frustration at not being able to understand or communicate.

Anne Sullivan came to live with the Keller family in Tuscumbia, Alabama, in 1886 and started to teach Helen.

This extract from Helen's autobiography reveals the moment when she learned that all things have names. This was the first step in learning a language that would help her to communicate.

- Read and enjoy autobiography set in a different time and culture
- Recognize the structure and main features of autobiography
- Explore how setting and character are developed
- Work out the meaning of new words
- Develop a wide vocabulary through reading

First lessons in life

I felt approaching footsteps, I stretched out my hand as I supposed to my mother. Someone took it, and I was caught up and held close in the arms of her who had come to reveal all things to me, and, more than all things else, to love me.

5   The morning after my teacher came she led me into her room and gave me a doll. When I had played with it a little while, Miss Sullivan slowly spelled into my hand the letters d-o-l-l. I was at once interested in this finger play and tried to imitate it. When I finally succeeded in making the letters correctly, I was
10 filled with pleasure and pride. Running downstairs to my mother I held up my hand and made the letters for 'doll'. I did not know that I was spelling a word or even that words existed; I was simply making my fingers go in monkey-like imitation. In the days that followed I learned to spell in this way a great many
15 words, among them 'pin', 'hat', 'cup' and a few verbs like 'sit', 'stand' and 'walk'. But my teacher had been with me several weeks before I understood that everything has a name.

One day, while I was playing with my new doll, Miss Sullivan put my big rag doll into my lap also, spelled d-o-l-l and tried to
20 make me understand that d-o-l-l applied to both. Earlier in the day we had had a tussle over the words m-u-g and w-a-t-e-r. Miss Sullivan had tried to impress it upon me that m-u-g is 'mug' and that w-a-t-e-r is 'water', but I persisted in confusing

Helen Keller, aged eight, with her teacher Anne Sullivan, in 1888

Glossary

reveal make (previously unknown or secret) information known to others

persisted continued thinking or doing something in spite of difficulty or opposition

25 the two. In despair, she had dropped the subject for the time being, only to take it up again at the first opportunity. I became impatient at her repeated attempts and, seizing the new doll, I dashed it upon the floor. I was delighted when I felt the fragments of the broken doll at my feet. I had not loved the doll. In the still, dark world in which I lived, there was no

30 strong sentiment or feelings of tenderness.

I felt my teacher sweep the fragments to one side of the hearth, and I had a sense of satisfaction that the cause of my discomfort was removed. She brought me my hat, and I knew I was going out into the warm sunshine. This thought, if a wordless sensation

35 may be called a thought, made me hop and skip with pleasure.

We walked down the path to the well-house, attracted by the fragrance of the honeysuckle with which it was covered. Someone was drawing water and my teacher placed my hand under the spout. As the cool stream gushed over one hand she

40 spelled into the other the word 'water', first slowly, then rapidly. I stood still, my whole attention fixed upon the motions of her fingers.

Suddenly the mystery of language was revealed to me. I knew then that w-a-t-e-r meant the wonderful cool something that

45 was flowing over my hand. That living word awakened my soul, gave it light, hope, joy, set it free! There were barriers still, it is true, but barriers that could in time be swept away.

I left the well-house eager to learn. Everything had a name, and each name gave birth to a new thought. As we returned

50 to the house every object which I touched seemed to quiver with life. That was because I saw everything with the strange, new sight that had come to me. On entering the door I remembered the doll I had broken. I felt my way to the hearth and picked up the pieces.

55 I tried to put them together. Then my eyes filled with tears; for I realized what I had done, and for the first time I felt repentance and sorrow.

From *The Story of My Life* by HELEN KELLER

- Read and enjoy autobiography set in a different time and culture
- Recognize the structure and main features of autobiography
- Explore how setting and character are developed
- Work out the meaning of new words
- Contribute to group discussions and build on others' ideas

Glossary

dashed threw with great force
fragments small pieces
sentiment feelings of tenderness, sadness or nostalgia
tenderness gentle kindness
hearth floor of a fireplace
quiver tremble or shake with a slight, quick motion
repentance feeling of regret or remorse
sorrow deep sadness

?

Imagine you are both visually impaired and hard of hearing like Helen Keller. Contemplate how that would impact your daily life and your ability to move from place to place. Would you be able to live the same life you have now? How do you think your friends and family would react? And what about other people's attitudes towards you?

Comprehension

A

1 Why is learning language more of a challenge for Helen than for others?

2 What basic things does Helen not understand?

3 What else is lacking in Helen's 'still, dark world'?

4 What is the significance of the smashed doll?

B

1 Write a definition for the following words and phrases:
   • 'imitate' (line 8)
   • 'applied to both' (line 20)
   • 'impress it upon me' (line 22)
   • 'rapidly' (line 40).

2 Find the words in the text which mean the same as the following:
   • coming near (line 1)
   • to reach out (line 1)
   • perfume (line 37)
   • flowed (line 39)
   • movement (line 41).

3 Why does Helen call her first steps in learning the words 'monkey-like imitation'? (line 13)

4 What does the 'mystery of language' refer to? (line 43)

5 What phrase in paragraph 4 (lines 31–35) highlights the connection between learning a language and learning to talk about ideas?

C

1 Why is learning to use language so important? Do you think that learning to communicate is the most important life skill? Why? Why not?

2 Imagine what it is like to grow up not being able to learn from other people by listening to what they say and watching what they do. How else might you learn about the world?

Stretch zone

Write a sentence to show the meaning of each word or phrase from comprehension question B1. Example: 'I tried to imitate my father's angry voice.'

Have a go at using braille

By the age of ten, Helen was a proficient braille reader. Braille is a form of written language for blind people, where letters are represented by patterns of raised dots that are felt with the fingertips.

Look at the braille alphabet below, then write your name in braille. You will have to represent the raised dots with just a pen on paper, so make sure you put each dot in the correct place.

Write a short message to your partner. Then see if they can work out what you have written.

A blind person's fingertips 'read' the raised dots on a page of braille.

BRAILLE ALPHABET

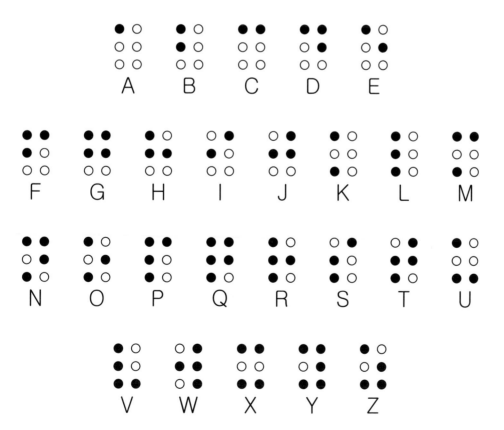

English braille alphabet. The black dots are raised so that fingertips can feel them.

- Develop a wide vocabulary through reading
- Use strategies to work out the meaning of unfamiliar words
- Use context in the text to identify word class

Helping people communicate: modern technology

In the last few decades, thanks to advances in modern technology, people with impaired vision can do numerous things more easily than before such as writing documents, browsing the internet, and sending and receiving emails. Screen-reading

5 software, and special talking and braille devices, allow people with no or little vision to use computers and other electronic devices independently. This technology – commonly known as assistive or adaptive technology – is continually evolving, and has removed many access barriers for people with impaired

10 vision.

These days, smartphones and tablets have further revolutionized the way people who are blind or visually impaired interact with and use technology. By using a special app, visually impaired people can take a picture of a print letter and their

15 phone will read it out loud within a matter of seconds. There is no need for bulky tape recorders any more. With another app, books can be downloaded in a matter of seconds onto a tablet and listened to immediately. And it's not just visually impaired people who find this technology useful. Audio

20 books are popular among sighted people too.

Learning tip
To work out the meaning of unfamiliar words, look at the rest of the sentence (the context) and especially the parts before and after the unfamiliar word. It might help to identify the word class. What is the relationship between the words and how are they are being used? For example, if the unfamiliar word comes before an object (a noun), could it be an adjective?

Comprehension

B

1 Look at the words below, taken from the text. Use the context of each word to match it with the correct word class and correct meaning.

Word from text	Word class	Meaning
browsing	adverb	conditions or obstacles that prevent movement or access to something
software	preposition	too big and taking up too much space
commonly	noun	inside (something such as a time limit)
continually	verb	programs and other operating information used by a computer
barriers	adverb	very often; frequently
within	adjective	looking at something in a leisurely and casual way
bulky	noun	repeated frequently in the same way; regularly

Explore the power of touch

You have found out how important touch is to blind people in learning to read words through braille. A braille reader literally touches the raised dots to 'read' the letters. The following poem is about the non-literal, or metaphorical, meanings of to 'touch' and to be 'touched'.

- Discuss the features of different types of poems
- Discuss how poets play with themes and conventions
- Explain how language features create effects

Touching

This is a song
About touch and touching.
You touch me – a way of feeling.
I touch you – a way of understanding.
5   We are touched
By a film or a book.
We are touched
When a stranger is kind.
How can we live
10   Without touching and being touched?

There is a healing touch,
It makes the sick whole again.
Let's keep in touch
We say to a friend who's going away.
15   To have the right touch
Means to know how it's done.
Touching is an art,
It's the movement
To and from the heart.

20   Some are easily touched.
Some are hard to touch.
You are often touched.
I am often touched.

NISSIM EZEKIEL

Language tip
Many verbs have a **literal** and a **non-literal** meaning. For example, the literal meaning of 'touch' is 'to put the fingertips in contact with something in order to feel it'.

For example: 'The blind girl touched the raised dots in her braille book to read the story.'

The non-literal meaning of 'touch' is 'to have an emotional effect'. It is often used in the passive form.

For example: 'I was touched by all the kindness I received when I was ill.'

'We are touched by a film or a book.'

Comprehension

1 Which lines describe the difference between the inward movement of being touched by something or someone, and the outward movement of reaching out to someone else?

2 Which lines link being touched in both a physical and in an emotional way?

3 Which lines refer to the relationship between the reader and the writer?

1 Copy the table below. Use a dictionary to complete the table of idioms using the word 'touch'.

Idiom	Meaning
finishing touch	
	unaware of recent changes or events
a soft touch	easily persuaded
lose one's touch	
	a risky situation where you are uncertain of the outcome
touch down	

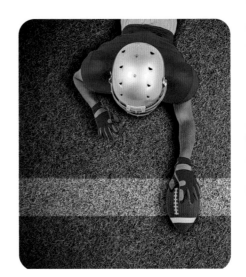

2 What is the difference between someone being touched and someone being touchy?

3 What does the poet mean by having the 'right touch'? (line 15)

1 How is a person touched by art or literature?

2 Which story from a book or film do you find the most touching?

3 How is being touched by a scene in a book or film different from being touched by something a person you know does for you in real life?

What touches you?

Choose the line or two lines from the poem which you like the best. Think of an experience which fits the lines. It could be a personal experience or the experience of someone you know or have read about. You can also be creative and just make up an experience!

Write down your chosen line or lines from the poem and an account of the experience which fits the lines.

Communicating with animals

The writer of the following account is J.H. Williams, who was known as 'Elephant Bill'. He was an English vet who looked after and had great empathy for the elephants in the teak forests of Myanmar in the 1930s (when it was called Burma). The elephants were used to move the heavy logs in the forests.

In the text, Elephant Bill describes his experience with a female elephant called Ma Kyaw.

- Read and enjoy autobiography set in a different time and culture
- Recognize the structure and main features of autobiography
- Work out the meaning of new words

The elephant who spoke to me

I know that an elephant can be grateful for relief from pain and sickness. I remember one elephant, Ma Kyaw. She had terrible lacerations on her back caused by a tiger's claws, and I treated her every day for three weeks. To begin with she
5 suffered great pain and made a lot of fuss. But I was determined to treat her and she became a good patient. When she was sufficiently healed I sent her back to camp with her rider, and gave instructions that she was to be given light dressings of fly repellent on the wounds.

10 I later on had the chance to inspect her. She was the last in the row of elephants and I went over her back very carefully, kneading the wounds with my hands. I found one little hole which still suppurated. There was great tenderness along a line about nine inches long where the wound had healed over. It
15 was undoubtedly infected. Ma Kyaw let me open it up to its full length there and then, although it obviously gave her great pain.

I did not see her again for two months. I was having a cup of tea in camp outside my tent, while seven elephants were being
20 washed in the river nearby ready for me to inspect them. The animals started to come out of the river and to return to camp to dry off before my inspection. The last elephant was Ma Kyaw with her rider following her on foot. As she passed me about fifty yards away, I called out. I did so to greet the rider
25 and to show that I had recognized him. "How is Ma Kyaw's back?" I called.

Map showing Myanmar in Southeast Asia

Glossary

lacerations deep cuts or tears in skin or flesh

dressings pieces of material used to cover and protect a wound

kneading massaging or squeezing with the hands

suppurated formed/ discharged pus; festered

infected contaminated with harmful organisms

33

Her rider did not hear me, but Ma Kyaw swung round, at right angles to the way she was going, and came towards me. She walked straight up to where I was sitting. I patted her on the
30 trunk and gave her a banana from my table. Then, without any word of command, she dropped into the sitting position and leaned right over towards me, so as to show me her back. Having patted her, I told her, "Tah" (get up), and away she went. I was sure that she had come to say "thank you". Then
35 I began to think that perhaps she had come to see me merely because she remembered my voice.

This made me think over the incident again. Perhaps she came and showed me her back in order to tell me that it was still painful. But I am sure that she liked me, trusted me, and was
40 gratful – and that we were very good friends.

From *Elephant Bill* by J.H. Williams

An elephant working in the teak forests of Myanmar

Comprehension

1 What evidence is there that Ma Kyaw's wound was very serious?
2 Why do you think the elephants need a vet to look after them?
3 What kind of work do elephants do in Myanmar?
4 How did the writer know that Ma Kyaw's wounds were still infected?
5 What did the elephant do on their next meeting that showed she trusted the vet?

1 What are 'lacerations'? (line 3) What caused them? How do we know the elephant was in pain from the lacerations?
2 What is another word for 'suppurated'? (line 13)
3 Find three adverbs or adverbial phrases in the first paragraph. Identify if they refer to when, how long or how often.

1 Why do you think it was necessary for the vet to inspect the elephants regularly and for the elephants to be washed before the inspection?
2 How would you describe the relationship between Ma Kyaw and the vet? Do you think the elephant knew the vet was trying to help her?
3 The writer is not certain what Ma Kyaw was trying to communicate. What did he think the elephant might be saying?
4 Can you think of any other stories or films where animals and humans help one another?

Write a report

Work in small groups. Imagine that you are Elephant Bill and you have to write a report on Ma Kyaw. Discuss what you would write. Use the following subheadings to help you and make notes of each other's ideas:

- My treatment of Ma Kyaw
- Ma Kyaw's behaviour
- My conclusions

Use your notes to write your own report. Use adverbs and adverbial phrases to say when, how long and how often the treatment took place.

When you have finished writing, proofread and edit your reports in pairs. Use a dictionary or the internet to check your spelling.

- Use implicit and explicit evidence from the text to answer questions
- Understand how texts reflect when and where they were written
- Explore how setting and character are developed
- Write a report, using a range of sentence features
- Proofread and edit a report

Language tip
Adverbs and adverbial phrases of time change or add meaning to a sentence by telling us when, for how long and how often an action happened. For example:

When: 'I'm going on holiday with my friends tomorrow.'

How long: 'We're going away for one week.'

How often: 'I'll ring home every night to let my parents know I'm okay.'

 Stretch zone

Write a short personal account of an experience in which you were able to communicate without using words. Why do you think it is important to be able to communicate on this level?

Why don't we all have enough to eat?

> ' Ending world hunger is one of the greatest challenges of our times '
>
> WORLD FOOD PROGRAMME

Talk about ...

- Do you agree with what the World Food Programme says about ending world hunger?
- Who is responsible for ending world hunger? Why?
- What do you think causes food shortage?

In some parts of the world, people do not have enough to eat. Some are even dying from lack of food, poor nutrition and famine.

International agencies collect statistics on poverty and hunger around the world. These statistics can be used as a tool for trying to make sure that help goes where it is needed and where resources are scarce. Statistics also monitor areas where poverty and hunger are being reduced or are increasing. Unfortunately, in recent years, both poverty and hunger have been increasing.

Word origins

famine (n), from the Latin word *fames*, meaning 'hunger'
Related word:
- famished

- Read texts, study maps and express opinions
- Communicate personal opinions confidently

Hunger around the world keeps rising

Globally, 1 in 9 people are hungry or undernourished – that's about 768 million people going to bed hungry every night.

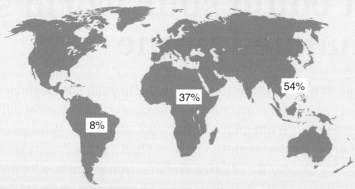

37%

54%

8%

99% of people suffering from undernourishment live in less developed and developing countries: 54% in Asia, 37% in Africa and 8% in Latin America and the Caribbean.

- The main drivers of hunger are:

War and conflict

Natural disasters

Extreme weather conditions and climate change

Pandemics

Gender and education inequality

Poverty

Poor farming practices and extravagant food waste

- About 60% of people living in hunger are women.
- About 3.1 million children die from undernutrition every year.

And yet ...
- The world produces 1.5 times enough food to feed everyone on the planet right now. It also already produces enough food to feed the estimated 10 billion population of the world in 2050.
- The United Nations estimates that about 17% of global food production is wasted.
- 1 in 3 adults and children around the world are overweight and 13% of adults are obese.

Talk about ...
- Do these facts shock you? Which are the most shocking facts?
- What are the main causes of world hunger? Do you think many people go hungry in your country/ region?
- If we are producing more than 1.5 times enough food to feed everyone, where do you think all the extra food goes? What can we do to solve the problem of food waste?

Stretch zone

What do you think are the main causes of food waste? What can be done so that we waste a lot less food? List your ideas for how we can reduce food waste in supermarkets, restaurants, schools and/or in the home.

- Recognize the structure and main features of a newspaper article
- Develop a wide vocabulary through reading
- Work out the meaning of new words

Drought in Madagascar

Read the newspaper report about the situation in southern Madagascar where years of drought have caused severe famine. Then answer the questions that follow.

Severe drought could spur world's first climate change famine

Over one million people in Madagascar are struggling to get enough to eat, due to what could become the first famine caused by climate change, according to the World Food Programme (WFP).

The region has been hit hard by successive years of severe drought, forcing families in rural communities to resort to desperate measures just to survive. Madagascar, the fourth largest island in the world, has a unique ecosystem which includes animals and plants found nowhere else on the planet. The country experiences a dry season, usually from May to October, followed by a rainy season that starts in November.

"However, climate change has upset the cycle, affecting smallholder farmers and their neighbours," said Alice Rahmoun, WFP Communications Officer, speaking to UN News on Thursday. "There is of course less rain, so when there is the first rain, they can maybe have hope and sow some seeds. But one little rainfall is not a proper rainy season," she said. "So there's not enough rain, so harvests fail constantly, so people have nothing to harvest and nothing to renew their food stocks and nothing to eat."

Ms Rahmoun was recently in southern Madagascar, where WFP and partners are supporting hundreds of thousands of people through short- and long-term assistance. "The effect of the drought differs from place to place," she said. While some communities have not had a proper rainy season for three years, the situation might be a lot worse 100 kilometres away. She recalled seeing villages surrounded by dried-out fields, and tomato plants which were completely brown from lack of water.

In some areas, where they are still able to plant something, they are trying to grow crops such as sweet potatoes and beans. Though in other areas, absolutely nothing is growing, so people are just surviving by eating locusts, fruits and cactus leaves, but even the cactus are dying from the drought.

WFP is collaborating with humanitarian partners, and the Malagasy government, to provide two types of response to the crisis. Some 700,000 people are receiving life-saving food aid, including supplementary products to prevent malnutrition.

"The second one is a more long-term response to allow local communities to be able to prepare for, respond to and recover from climate shocks better," said Ms Rahmoun. "So, this includes water projects. We're doing irrigation canals, reforestation and even micro-insurance to help smallholder farmers to recover from a lost harvest, for example."

3C Non-fiction Comprehension

Comprehension

A

1 What is different about this famine from others?

2 Which charity does the interviewee work for?

3 What are some people eating to supplement their diets?

4 Explain what is meant by 'short-term and long-term assistance'.

B

1 What is the purpose of the first paragraph (in bold)? Explain (with supporting quotations from the extract) how this report gives the who, where, what, when, and why of the story.

2 Which subheading in the box below is most appropriate for each of these sections of the text?
- Paragraphs 1 and 2
- Paragraph 3
- Paragraphs 4 and 5
- Paragraphs 6 and 7

> Varying impacts   Global warming and environment
> Providing life-saving aid   Daily life disrupted

3 Look at the first paragraph (in bold). Give one phrase that tells the reader that the information given is the opinion of someone else, not the writer.

4 What do you think the following phrases refer to:
  a 'desperate measures'? (line 8)
  b 'climate shocks'? (line 59)

5 Look at lines 25–30. The interviewee uses a well-known literary technique twice. Identify the technique and explain why she uses it. What effect is she trying to achieve?

C

1 Discuss why it is so important for WFP to offer both short-term and long-term assistance.

2 Do you know other ways that charities are trying to help regions or countries affected by drought, famine, natural disasters or conflict?

3 Why is it so important for developed countries to help other countries when they need it?

- Understand the structure and main features of a newspaper article
- Work out the meaning of new words
- Explain how language features create effects
- Identify the viewpoint of the writer and distinguish between fact and opinion

Glossary

struggling finding it very hard to achieve or get something

assistance provision of money, resources or information to help someone

collaborating working jointly on an activity or project

supplementary completing or enhancing something

malnutrition lack of proper nutrition, caused by not having enough to eat

Language tip
Repeating something three times (called the **rule of three**) adds emphasis to the writer's point of view or message.

For example, 'It's good; it's wholesome; it's the best!'

No one knows why the rule of three works, but it is scientifically proven to be stronger than a list of two or four items, for example. The effect has even more impact if the words chosen are more emotional or stronger as the list builds up.

- Research a topic from different sources and make notes
- Discuss research findings
- Write text in question and answer form

Who gives food aid?

Look at these logos from some of the international aid organizations and charities which help people all over the world. The organizations help people who are victims of war, drought and other natural disasters, sickness and homelessness.

In your group, choose one of these organizations to research. Divide your research up so that each person reports on a specific area in answer to the following questions:

- Where is the organization based? How many offices does it have? How many people does it employ worldwide? Write short biographies on two or three individuals and their roles within the organization.
- How is the organization financed? How does it raise money? How much money does it need? Give examples of the contributions raised by individual donor countries.
- How does the organization distribute aid? Give examples of how transport and distribution problems affect its programmes.
- What recent aid relief has the organization provided? Give some examples of recent campaigns and countries it helped.

When you have completed your research, discuss and share your findings with the group. Take notes on the rest of the group's research findings.

Write frequently asked questions (FAQs)

Use the information your group has found to write FAQs about how your chosen organization contributes to relieving world hunger. You may use some of the topic questions above as your headings so that they look like FAQs. For example, if you chose the charity Oxfam, your first two headings could be:

How does Oxfam relieve hunger?

Where is Oxfam based?

If you can, include pictures and logos.

WFP

World Food Programme

World Food Programme (WFP) is part of the United Nations

Save the Children Fund

Oxfam

Oxfam (the short form of Oxford Famine Relief)

Médecins Sans Frontières (Doctors Without Borders in English)

International Federation of Red Cross and Red Crescent Societies

Create a logo

A logo is a graphic design, emblem or symbol used to make sure people quickly recognize a particular organization. The logo may include a picture which clearly represents something specific, a symbol or just be an abstract shape. It may include the name or initials of the organization it represents, or it may not. Most importantly, a logo must be distinctive and memorable.

You are going to create a new organization which aims to end food waste in your country. This waste could be in the home or in supermarkets, restaurants, cinemas, hotels, or another business which uses food. Create a logo for this organization, following the steps below.

1 Choose a specific purpose and suitable name for your organization.

2 Think about the main characteristic that represents your organization's aims.

3 Get designing. Divide a sheet of A4 paper into six or more boxes. Create a different logo design in each box, taking inspiration from the following ideas:

- a picture, symbol or shape that sums up your organization's spirit
- the organization's name or initials
- a bright colour scheme of no more than four colours
- the shape and the colour of the text.

Consider how different colours work with each other. Logos often use bright, primary colours or colours on the opposite side of the colour wheel, as these have the most visual impact.

4 Decide on your favourite design. If you cannot decide, ask a partner for feedback.

5 Try making small amendments, for example, to the colour scheme or the way you write the letters.

6 Make a final copy of your logo to add to a class display.

Talk about ...

According to a report by a food magazine, supermarkets waste 100,000 tonnes of edible food annually in the UK alone. In fact, it's estimated that the UK's total food waste could feed upwards of 30 million people a year. Do you think this is right? Are supermarkets or consumers to blame for this waste? What can supermarkets do to prevent this waste?

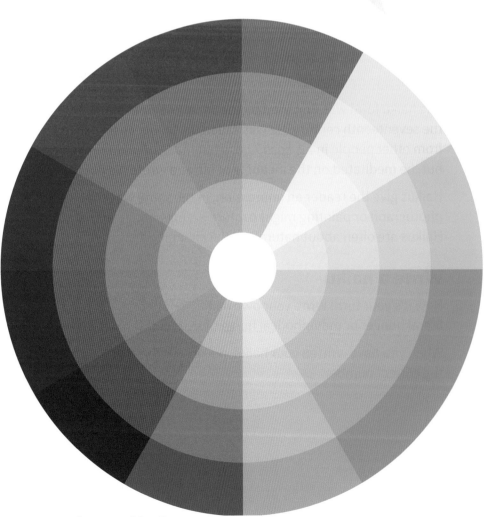

Logos use colour combinations that have high impact.

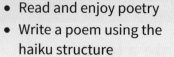

- Read and enjoy poetry
- Write a poem using the haiku structure

Impressions from haiku

Waiting for the lunchtime bell

My tummy rumbles
Focusing impossible
I am sooo hungry!

Hungry

I feel so hungry
I could eat a huge pizza
with extra toppings!

'Waiting for the lunchtime bell' and 'Hungry' are haikus. A haiku is a form of Japanese poetry that has a specific structure. It has just three lines and a total of 17 syllables, in the following pattern:

Line 1: Five syllables (my tum-my rum-bles)

Line 2: Seven syllables (foc-us-ing im-poss-i-ble)

Line 3: Five syllables (I am sooo hun-gry).

The lines do not rhyme.

The haiku form was first used by the Japanese poet Matsuo Bashō in the seventeenth century. He was called Bashō because he lived apart from other people in his *bashō-un*, a hut made of plantain leaves. In this hut, he meditated on the meaning of life and wrote his poetry.

Haikus give the reader an impression, in the same way that a photograph or painting might capture a single image of the world. Haikus are often about nature and the changing seasons.

Write a haiku

Now it's your turn! Write your own haiku about hunger. It can be about literal hunger or metaphorical hunger for something out of reach.

When you have written your haiku, make sure the syllables add up to the correct number.

Learning tip
A **syllable** is a unit of pronunciation with one vowel sound, with or without surrounding consonants. It can form the whole or part of a word. For example, there is one syllable in 'bridge' and two in 'crossing' and 'water'.

Word origins

haiku (n), comes from a contracted form of the Japanese *haikai no ku*, meaning 'light verse'

Fantasy fiction

The following extract comes from a fantasy story set a long time ago. Two young friends, Kate and Thomas, have spent a night out on the moors in Yorkshire, UK. When early morning comes, they are cold and extremely hungry. At Boggle Mill, they are unexpectedly treated to breakfast.

- Read and enjoy fiction
- Recognize the structure and main features of a narrative story
- Explore how setting and character are developed
- Develop a wide vocabulary through reading

Boggle Mill

Across the stream was a small stone cottage beside a mill, set higher up the bank and away from the water. It had a little vegetable garden to one side and several chickens scratched
5 away in the dirt. The door to the cottage was so small that a grown man would have to stoop to get in. It looked an inviting and friendly place, the smoke from its chimney indicating a warm fire inside. In the fresh morning light, it called Kate and Thomas to safety.

10 They could hear the sound of a man singing from inside.

Glossary

stoop bend one's head or body forwards and downwards
indicating pointing out; showing
spare have extra, more than needed

Language tip
Prepositional phrases
include both the preposition and the object that the preposition is referring to.

For example: 'Across the stream' (line 1)

'with a cloud of flour' (line 55)

Can you find any more examples in this unit?

A typical moorland scene

- Read and enjoy fiction
- Understand the structure and main features of a narrative story
- Explore how setting and character are developed
- Work out the meaning of new words

Suddenly the wooden door swung open and the contents of a saucepan were thrown on to the garden. The chickens rushed forwards. The man didn't notice Kate and Thomas by the fence as he scraped the rest of the chicken feed out of the saucepan

15 and went back inside. Thomas went up to the door and knocked three times on the dark wood. There was no reply. Thomas knocked again, hammering at the door with his fist.

"Hello. Can you spare some bread?" he shouted.

A small window to the side opened and the man's nose appeared.

20 "Please could we have some bread?" Thomas asked again.

The man looked at them through the window, examining them carefully.

"Well, if you want bread, you shall have it. You can't come to a mill and not find any bread, and some roast meat too. What about some tea?"

25 The window slammed shut, and the door opened. The man stared at Thomas and Kate covered in mud and stained with dirt.

"Come in, come in. You can't stand on the doorstep all day long. Come in out of the cold and warm yourselves by the fire."

30 The man spoke quickly and took them both into a large kitchen. A fire lit the whole room with a warm orange glow and scented the house with a smoky fragrance. There was a strong, sweet smell of fruitcake, and baking bread.

"Sit yourselves down, you both look like you've spent the night
35 outside. What are you doing here so early in the morning?" He stopped for a moment. "Oh, I'm Rueben, the miller, and this is my home." He held out his hands in friendship. "Welcome."

Rueben was a large man built like an ox. He had strong arms and broad shoulders and his hands were the size of shovels.
40 He wore a pair of old trousers, a shirt which had once been white, and a thick leather apron stained with flour. In fact, everything about him was stained with flour. His long white hair, his large ears, and even his thick, bushy eyebrows looked like freshly fallen snow. His big green eyes were smiling and

Glossary

slammed shut (a door, window or lid) forcefully and loudly

stained marked or discoloured with something that is not easily removed

Learning tip
Notice how the writer introduces the reader to Rueben gradually before giving a full description of his appearance. It can help to keep the audience interested if you introduce main characters gradually.

Language tip
Notice how the writer uses different senses to evoke a sense of warmth and comfort inside the large kitchen. He also uses long and complex sentences when describing the interior and Rueben's appearance.

45 warm and were the eyes of someone who could be trusted.

"Now let me get you that tea and some bread. You both look like you can do with something to warm you up."

Rueben opened the door of the oven and took out several thick slices of roast meat. He placed the hot meat on a plate and
50 gave it to them.

"Eat up and I'll get you some bread. Then you can tell me what you've been up to." Rueben took hold of a loaf of bread and broke it in half with his large hands. "Here you are. There's nothing like warm bread first thing in the morning."

55 He put the bread on the plate then clapped his hands, filling the air with a cloud of flour. They both began to eat, filling their mouths with the hot meat and bread as Rueben carried on with the morning's work. They watched as he swept the floor, and set the long wooden table in front of the small
60 window. Kate followed his every move but her mouth full of food made it impossible for her to speak.

Rueben had noticed the dirt on the children's boots, the stains and mud on their faces, and most of all their look of unease. His deep voice and broad accent made him sound like a stranger
65 to that part of the world.

"What are you doing out so early in these parts?" he asked. "We never get many visitors here to Boggle Mill."

From *Shadowmancer* by G.P. Taylor

- Use implicit and explicit evidence from the text to answer questions
- Explain how language features create effects
- Explain how setting and character is developed
- Write, proofread and edit a narrative story

Comprehension

1 What smells made the kitchen inviting?
2 Which words and phrases in the text tell you that Rueben was a big man?
3 What signs of Rueben's trade are there about him?
4 What particular feature of his appearance makes Rueben seem like a friendly man?

1 Give an example of personification from the first paragraph.
2 Which bits of the text reveal Rueben's initial caution about inviting the children into his home? Why do you think he behaves this way?
3 How does Rueben later demonstrate his kindness and concern for the children?
4 Why do you think Kate 'followed his every move'? (line 59)

1 What role does food play in this story? How does it represent safety as well as hospitality and charity?
2 What role does food play in special family gatherings and celebrations in your country?
3 Why do we sometimes treat people who are different with suspicion?

Write a story about meeting someone new

Write a story about meeting someone who appears to be quite extraordinary at first, but who then manages to put you at ease.

- Describe the situation in detail. How did you meet? What were the circumstances that brought you together?
- Give a full account of your new friend's character through the things they say and do.
- What were your first impressions of this person? How did your opinion of them change?
- Write about what you gained from the experience.

When you have finished, use a dictionary to proofread and edit your story.

Stretch zone

Proofread and edit your partner's story. Explain what you like most about their story and suggest some ways they can improve their narrative.

- Read fiction set in a different time and culture
- Work out the meaning of new words
- Identify how punctuation helps make meaning clear

A description good enough to eat!

When did you last appreciate a good meal because you were really, really hungry? In the following text, 12-year-old Dara and her family have fled from the war in Cambodia in the early 1980s. They have reached a refugee camp on the Thai–Cambodian border. In this extract, Dara and her family are eating rice. The description is short, but the words make it vivid.

What a wonderful thing

The fragrance of the long-grained rice was powerful. Steamy and sweet and warm, it wafted up to me. I had not seen such a generous mound of white rice for a long, long time.

5 I lifted a spoonful of rice and ate it. I thought about what a wonderful thing it is to eat rice. First you let the smell drift up in lazy spirals, sweet and elusive; then you look at the colour of it, softer and whiter than the surrounding steam. Carefully you put a spoonful in your mouth, and feel each grain separate on your tongue, firm and warm. Then you taste it – the rich 10 yet delicate sweetness of it. How different it was from the gritty red rice we'd been rationed for the last three years, gruel so bland and watery that it slipped right down your throat before you could even taste it. No, this was real rice, whole moist grains I could chew and savour.

From *The Clay Marble* by MINFONG HO

Glossary

vivid intensely deep or bright
mound rounded mass above a surface
elusive difficult to find, catch or achieve
rationed allowed to have only a fixed amount of something
gruel thin liquid food of oatmeal or other meal boiled in milk or water
savour taste (good food or drink) and enjoy it to the full

Language tip
To make the sentences flow smoothly and effectively while describing the rice experience, the writer uses punctuation such as a semi-colon (;) and a dash (–) to extend the length of the sentences.

Comprehension

1   Read the words and phrases below in the context of the text. Match each word or phrase to the correct definition.

Word or phrase	Meaning
'wafted' (line 2)	containing or covered with grit (tiny stones)
'drift' (line 5)	(of food or drink) unseasoned, mild-tasting or insipid
'lazy spirals' (line 6)	be carried slowly by a current of air or water
'grain' (line 8)	slowly making curved patterns
'gritty' (line 10)	(of a scent, sound, etc.) pass gently through the air
'bland' (line 12)	wheat or any other cultivated cereal used as food

2   When describing the experience of eating the rice, Dara refers to all of her senses except the sense of hearing. Give examples from the text of how each sense (sight, smell, taste and touch) is used to show how Dara enjoys eating the rice.

3   The writer uses repetition. Why?

4   Which other common literary techniques does the writer use? Give two examples from the first paragraph.

1   What does the long-grained rice mean to Dara after years of rationing? Do you think she might be feeling more hopeful for the future? Why or why not?

- Use implicit and explicit evidence from the text to answer questions
- Explain how language features create effects
- Understand how the senses are used to evoke vivid imagery
- Write descriptively using the senses to create vivid imagery
- Use literary devices to add impact, meaning and interest to writing

Language tip
When writing descriptive narrative, choose adjectives carefully to create appropriate imagery. Look at the range of adjectives used in Dara's description to describe white rice ('wonderful', 'firm' ...) and red rice ('gritty', 'bland' ...).

Describe your favourite food

Think of eating something that you really enjoy. Write a short and vivid description in a similar style to Dara's account of eating rice. Focus on your descriptive writing and aim to include:

- plenty of adjectives that describe the colour, texture, taste, smell and, if relevant, the temperature of the food
- any unique and special things about eating your chosen food
- adverbs to describe the way that you eat the food.

Historical fiction

The following story is about a 12-year-old boy called Eamonn and his family. It is set in the nineteenth century in Ireland, during the Irish Potato Famine. People in rural Ireland relied on potatoes as their staple food but, in 1846, disaster struck. The entire potato crop was ruined by potato blight. To make matters worse, English soldiers drove people from their homes. Those who had any money emigrated to America, but those who did not had to struggle to survive. One English soldier takes pity on Eamonn and gives him a gold sovereign, money which enables the family to rent a room. His father manages to find work, and Eamonn and his brother forage for food each day while his younger brother Shaun and baby sister stay with their mother.

Starving Irish people at the gates of a workhouse during the Irish potato famine

Hunger

Eamonn spent his days out with Dermot looking for any wild plants they could eat. His father was paid every evening and brought home enough money for one meal a day, but still the boys were always hungry.
5 They chewed on dandelion leaves to fool their stomachs into thinking they were getting a good meal, and took nettles home for their mother to make into soup. If they were lucky, a shopkeeper might give them an apple for doing an odd job for him, but every week there were fewer shopkeepers and more
10 hungry boys out looking for scraps to eat. A boy they met told them he once found a whole loaf of bread on someone's pile of rubbish. "There was only a bit of mould on it," he grinned. "You wouldn't believe what people throw out." After that, Dermot and Eamonn searched all the rubbish heaps every day,
15 but they never found anything to eat there. "We were daft to believe that boy," Dermot said. "No one would ever throw food away."

One night, less than two weeks after the canal works had been restarted, Dermot and Eamonn made their way home. They
20 had been out all day and hadn't found a single bit of food; nobody had any odd jobs for them to do either. It was after seven o'clock and they sat with Mammy and the two little ones in the dark room they had rented with the soldier's gold sovereign.

Glossary

potato blight kind of mould that affects potatoes
sovereign valuable gold coin
forage search a wide area to find something, such as edible wild mushrooms
dandelion, nettles wild plants
daft silly, stupid
odd job casual, small or one-off piece of work

- Read and enjoy fiction set in a different time and culture
- Recognize the main features of historical fiction
- Work out the meaning of new words

25 "Your Daddy will be home very soon," Mammy said to Shaun, "and then we'll all go out and have a feast with his wages."

Even Dermot knew that she was telling lies about the feast. Eamonn had noticed how his mother hardly ate anything at night time when they had their meal. She kept slipping spoonfuls 30 of coarse cornmeal porridge to Dermot and Shaun, and Eamonn saw how weary and ill she looked when they still said they were hungry. He always shook his head when she tried to give him her food.

He was old enough to know what the problem was. His father 35 was getting the same amount of money as he had been getting a few months ago, before they had stopped the works for a time, but the food now cost twice as much. And there were people who had enough money to pay three times as much as the asking price. Eamonn's parents bought less and less food 40 each week, and each week the price of cornmeal rose even higher.

They heard steps along the long hallway. "There's your Daddy now." Eamonn could tell, even in the dark, that his mother was smiling as she knew his arrival meant the arrival of more food.

45 Eamonn went to open the door and Shaun and Dermot catapulted past him, both wanting to be the first to give their father a hug. Usually Daddy threw them both up into the air, one after the other, but he wasn't in the mood for jokes. He patted them both on the head and touched Eamonn's cheek, "How are you, 50 boys?" Then he went over to the window and sat down with his back against the wall. It was a long time before he spoke.

"I didn't get my money today," he said. "There was no one there to pay out the wages."

Eamonn's mother sighed. "If it's no worse than that we'll 55 manage," she said. "We can manage until tomorrow."

No one came to pay the wages the next day, or the next. None of the men had been paid for a whole week, and still the money didn't come.

From *The Coldest Winter* by Elizabeth Lutzeier

Glossary

catapulted hurled or launched something

Comprehension

1 What did Eamonn and his brother go searching for every day?

2 What does it mean that Eamonn and his brother chewed leaves 'to fool their stomachs into thinking they were getting a good meal'? (lines 5–6)

3 Why does Eamonn's mother look 'weary and ill'? (line 31)

4 How did Eamonn's mother try to keep up her children's spirits?

5 How did the children feel when they heard their father's steps in the hallway?

6 In what way was their father's homecoming different on this day?

1 Look at line 51. What effect does the short sentence have?

2 Look at line 56 to the end. Explain how the writer uses language to show how serious the situation is.

1 Discuss what the 'problem' is that Eamonn is old enough to understand. Can you think of similar situations today?

2 Reread the last paragraph. How do you think Eamonn's father will be feeling? What do you think might happen next?

Perform a scene

In groups of four, act out the text from line 18 ('One night, less than two weeks after …') to the end. Take the roles of Mammy, Daddy, Eamonn and Eamonn's brother, Dermot. Pay attention to how you think your character must be feeling and try to communicate this through your performance. Choose an appropriate register (formal or informal) for your character and try to maintain it throughout. Show your performance to another group and watch theirs. Provide each other with feedback on how effectively setting and character were evoked.

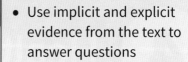
- Use implicit and explicit evidence from the text to answer questions
- Explore how setting and character are developed
- Communicate confidently in role-play
- Use the grammar and vocabulary of a register appropriate for purpose

Due to climate change, farmers in Colombia, who used to experience reliable rainfall, have been experiencing floods and drought. A knowledge exchange has been set up between them and Senegalese farmers, who have lots of experience and knowledge about farming during long periods of drought. What other ways could people work together on a global level to solve food crises and inequalities?

Stretch zone

Rewrite lines 42–58 ('They heard steps … money didn't come') in the mother's words and from her point of view. Add her thoughts and feelings.

Peasants struggling for food during the Irish Potato Famine

How can we all get the health care we need?

> **A healthy outside starts from the inside**

Talk about ...
- How do you stay healthy on the inside?
- Do you think much about your health and staying healthy or is it something you take for granted?
- Do you think it's true that people do not fully appreciate being healthy until they are sick?
- Why is having a healthy mind just as important as having a healthy body?

We all know that eating a balanced diet with lots of fruit and vegetables, drinking lots of water, doing plenty of exercise, and getting a good night's sleep keep our bodies healthy. But can you explain how the following activities help maintain a healthy lifestyle too?

- playing a few computer games with friends daily
- talking to friends regularly via chat groups
- meeting up with friends every so often to go to the cinema or a café
- buying yourself some nice clothes which fit you well
- always being kind and considerate to others
- caring about the community that you live in, for example always throwing your rubbish in a bin
- taking care of younger siblings or a pet
- giving some of your time to older people, such as grandparents.

Language tip
Words such as 'a lot', 'a few', 'some', and 'enough' can be used to describe the amount of things. They are called **quantifiers**.

Language tip
We use adverbs to say how often something happens. For example, 'hourly', 'daily', 'often', 'sometimes' and 'never'. These are called **adverbials of frequency**.

What are our human rights?

What do you know about the Universal Declaration of Human Rights? The 30 articles in the Declaration were agreed in 1948 by the United Nations. This Declaration sets out the rights and freedoms of human beings which should be protected all over the world.

> ❛Everybody has the right to a standard of living adequate for health and well-being of himself and his family, including food, clothing, housing and medical care❜
>
> Article 25 from the Universal Declaration of Human Rights, 1948

The picture below is an illustration of Article 25. The words of Article 25 could be simplified to: 'We all have a right to a home, enough money to live on and medical help if we are ill'. Look at the picture closely. Describe what you can see in detail. How many different climates and cultures can you see?

- Read texts and express opinions
- Discuss a topic using specialized vocabulary
- Communicate personal opinions confidently

Talk about ...

- Can you name any more of our human rights?
- Which do you think is the most important human right? Make sure you justify your answer.

?

Imagine that your only source of water is a well ten miles away from home. What impact would this have on the amount of water you use daily? How do you think the lack of access to water would affect you personally and also your community?

Unclean water

Every year worldwide, several million children under the age of five die of diarrhoea. Diarrhoea is one of the major causes of death in babies and young children in places that do not have clean water to drink. In many parts of the world, people depend on water which is contaminated. Water can be contaminated by human and animal waste, and drainage from fields or seawater.

In serious cases of dehydration, an intravenous drip is used to help the body absorb fluids and medicine.

How to make a rehydration remedy

Diarrhoea is particularly dangerous for children, as it can quickly drain the body of essential fluids, causing dehydration. Many children could be saved if a simple rehydration remedy was given to them. This diagram shows how to make a rehydration remedy with sugar and salt. Why do you think it has been designed this way? Do you think it would be easy to follow?

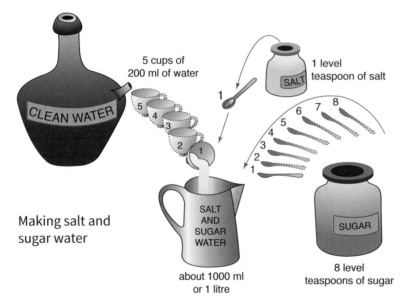

5 cups of 200 ml of water

1 level teaspoon of salt

CLEAN WATER

Making salt and sugar water

SALT AND SUGAR WATER

about 1000 ml or 1 litre

SUGAR

8 level teaspoons of sugar

Now look at another set of instructions below describing how to make a rehydration remedy with salt and sugar water. Explain why these instructions are not very useful.

> You should try to find a largish jug and fill it with clean water. Then all you need to do is add a little salt and lots and lots of sugar. After that you can give the mixture a good stir.

Glossary

diarrhoea condition when you defecate too frequently and in liquid form

contaminated made impure by pollution or poison

drainage process of water and other liquids flowing into pipes, rivers or the ground

absorb to take in or soak up liquid

rehydration restoring of fluid into something

remedy medicine or treatment for a disease or injury

Word origins

dehydration (n), meaning 'loss or removal of water', comes from the ancient Greek word *hydor*, meaning 'water'

Related words:
- rehydration
- hydro-electric

intravenous (adj), meaning 'having a substance put into a vein', comes from the Latin words *intra*, meaning 'within, inside', and *vena*, meaning 'vein'

Write clear instructions

Use the diagram on page 54 to help you to write a clear set of instructions for making salt and sugar water.

- You will need to be very precise about the way it should be made and the amounts of each ingredient.
- Use the same approach as you would for writing a recipe. (Include instructions like the importance of sterilizing the container and washing your hands.)
- When you have finished writing, proofread your instructions and correct any mistakes in grammar, punctuation or spelling.

Describe a bicycle

Now you will use what you have learned about writing clear instructions to teach your partner how to draw a bicycle. First, explain the various features of a bicycle, making your description very detailed. The following words will help you: 'handlebar', 'basket', 'bell', 'pedal', 'brake lever', 'spoke', 'hub', 'reflector', 'mudguard', 'saddle'.

Now look at the four simple steps below for drawing a bicycle. Add a written instruction for each diagram. When you have finished, swap with a partner. Read your partner's instructions to check they make sense.

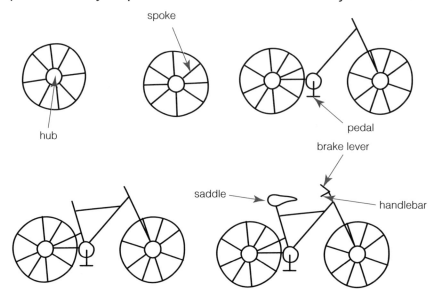

A bicycle is sometimes called a 'bike' for short. Some people attach trailers to their bicycles to help them carry equipment, supplies and even other people. What other kinds of 'cycles' can you think of?

Stretch zone

Work in pairs. Draw a very simple picture (for example, of a house) without letting a partner see it. Give clear, simple instructions for your partner to draw the same picture. Compare the two pictures. Change roles and repeat the exercise. How could you improve your instructions?

- Write instructions on how to do things
- Use the imperative to write instructions

Language tip

An **imperative sentence** is used to make a command or direct someone to do something. For example, for your instructions, you could write: 'Take a jar of clean water'. Putting the verb 'take' first turns that sentence into a command. Note that an imperative sentence does not require a subject; the pronoun 'you' is implied.

Learning tip

For accurate spelling, it helps to know that a single word can be converted into different forms. For example, the word 'contaminate' can be used as a verb in 'to contaminate'. It can also become an adjective, 'contaminated', or a noun, 'contamination'.

Word origins

bicycle (n), comes from the Latin word *bi*, meaning 'two' and the Greek word *kylos*, meaning 'circle' or 'wheel'
Related words:
- binoculars
- bisect
- tricycle
- unicycle

How can a bicycle help?

Emily Wille is a midwife (a birth attendant) in Malawi, in Africa. She often has to ride her bicycle to patients when they cannot come to the two-roomed hut behind her home, where she holds a weekly antenatal clinic for pregnant women. Sometimes the babies are delivered here or at their homes. If there are complications, Emily refers them to the Mlambe Hospital in Lunzu.

The charity World Vision supports Emily, and others like her, with training and equipment – including a bicycle ambulance. Before the bicycle was available, pregnant mothers in Emily's remote community were often taken to their nearest birth attendant by wheelbarrow!

Emily holds two of the babies delivered at her village clinic.

Emily takes a patient to the maternity clinic by bicycle ambulance.

Objectives

- Understand the development of ideas and themes in a text
- Communicate confidently in role-play
- Use verbal and non-verbal techniques to present the role convincingly

Be an interviewer

Work in groups of three or four. Imagine that a local newspaper in Malawi runs an article each week called 'Heroes in the community'. This week they want to interview Emily Wille about her job.

One of you will be the interviewer and the others will be Emily and the people in the community she has helped. The interviewer needs to interview everyone for the article. The roles are:

- interviewer
- Emily Wille
- a pregnant woman who had difficulties and needed to be transported by Emily to hospital
- a pregnant woman who needed Emily's help very quickly to deliver her twins.

Word origins

antenatal (adj), comes from the Latin words, *ante*, meaning 'before', and *natus*, meaning 'having been born'. Pregnant women attend antenatal classes and clinics to check on the health of their unborn babies and to prepare to give birth.

Related words:

- anticipate
- antique
- nature
- nation

Pedal power

It is not just countries in Africa that use bicycle power to support community health. These days, many other countries use bicycles to transport hospital supplies and to help medical staff to get around. Bicycle ambulances often get to people more quickly when there are accidents at crowded public events.

There is a growing campaign worldwide to learn from the example of developing countries, like Malawi, and go back to using bicycles instead of cars.

Organizations like the World Cycling Alliance, which has members all over the world, has the following mission statement: **To promote cycling as a mode of transport (including leisure and touristic cycling) for the benefit of people worldwide**. The Alliance runs many projects and initiatives urging governments to improve street safety for cyclists and to support the use of bicycles as a serious form of transport.

- Select formal or informal registers and vocabulary which are appropriate for the purpose and audience
- Know when to use Standard English and Non-Standard English
- Write from a particular point of view

Write a letter in support of improving bicycle infrastructure

Write a letter to your local government representative in support of the World Cycling Alliance. In your letter, you could request that more cycle paths are created, or more bike lanes on main roads, so that people can ride bikes safely.

Make a list of all the reasons why riding a bike is good for you. In your letter, focus on the benefits of riding a bike for people in your community. Also focus on the impact this has on the rest of the world.

> Dear ... ,
> I live in ... and would like the ... local government to put in more bike paths. Cycling is great fun, and helps to keep people fit and healthy ...

How to fix broken bones

The following extract is from Shusha Guppy's memoir *The Blindfold Horse*, which describes memories of her childhood in the 1940s. Shusha was born in Tehran, which is the capital city of Iran, a country that was then called Persia. When she broke her arm, her mother took her to the bone-setter in the bazaar. He was a potter, but he had also been treating sprains and broken bones for years.

- Read and enjoy a memoir set in a different time and culture
- Work out the meaning of new words

Word origins

bazaar (n), comes from the Farsi word *bãzãr*, meaning 'market' (Farsi is the Indo-European language spoken in Iran and Afghanistan)

manipulate (v), comes from the Latin word *manus*, meaning 'hand'
Related words:
- manufacture   • manual

A turquoise-glazed ceramic tile from Iran

A visit to the bone-setter

One day, when I was about eleven or twelve the telephone rang and I ran to answer it. I caught my leg in the carpet and fell down the stairs, landing on my wrist. It looked broken, hurt badly, and swelled immediately. My mother took me to the
5   bazaar to see Mashdi Habib, the bone-setter. He had a pottery shop in the potters' section where he sold ceramics from his native Hamadan in the north-west of Persia: bowls, jugs, plates, tiles, crockery of all sorts. They were earthenware, or glazed with ornamental patterns, above all in the famous turquoise-
10   blue of his region.

Bone-setting was his hobby and he was so skilled that his reputation had spread far beyond the bazaar. Even when a bone was broken into many pieces he could make it whole again. He practised his skill on broken pottery. He used to
15   break a jug into a dozen pieces, put them in a sack, and from the outside manipulate the pieces into place like a jigsaw puzzle!

- Read and enjoy a memoir set in a different time and culture
- Work out the meaning of new words

Mashdi Habib was sitting on a stool outside his shop when we arrived. On seeing us, he got up, bowed courteously and motioned us inside. With infinite gentleness he manipulated my wrist and said that it was not broken but only slightly cracked and that he could soon put it right. He took some warm ashes from the brazier and poured them into a cotton bag, then wrapped the bag around my wrist. If the bone had been broken he would have kept it motionless by putting it between two strips of wood, after manipulating it into place and covering it with hot ashes. He then tore a piece of rag from a sheet and made me a sling, saying: "Keep it still for a couple of days. In a week your wrist will be as good as new!"

A whole chapter could be written on the use of ashes in Persia's traditional folk-medicine: they are the antiseptic of the poor even today. Before the antibiotic penicillin was easily available, ashes were used to treat cuts, sterilize wounds, ease rheumatic pains and much more. Alas, Mashdi Habib and the other bone-setters all eventually disappeared with the development of modern methods of surgery and plaster-casting in dealing with broken bones.

From *The Blindfold Horse* by SHUSHA GUPPY

Glossary

swelled became larger or rounder in size

crockery plates, dishes, cups and other similar items

glazed covered with a smooth, shiny coating or finish

brazier portable heater consisting of a pan or stand for holding lighted coals

sterilize make something free from bacteria or germs

wounds injuries

A pottery workshop in modern-day Hamadan, Iran

Comprehension

A

1 Why did the writer's mother take Shusha to the bone-setter rather than to a doctor?

2 How did Mashdi Habib practise his bone-setting skills?

3 How did Mashdi Habib's treatment of a broken bone differ from his treatment of a cracked bone?

4 What advice did Mashdi Habib give to Shusha?

B

1 Find the following words in the text:
- an adjective in paragraph 1 which means 'where he was born'
- a verb in paragraph 2 which means 'control something in a skilful manner'
- a noun in paragraph 3 which means 'a device to limit movement of the shoulder or elbow while it heals'
- a mass noun in paragraph 4 which means 'people without sufficient money to live at a standard considered comfortable'.

2 What does the adverb 'courteously' tell you about the way Mashdi Habib treated Shusha and her mother? (line 18)

3 What does the phrase 'with infinite gentleness' tell you about the way Mashdi Habib treated Shusha's wrist? (line 19)

C

1 Have you, or someone you know, ever been injured in an accident? Was the injury just a small scrape or quite serious? Describe what happened and how.

- Understand how texts reflect when and where they were written
- Understand how setting and characters are developed
- Use implicit and explicit evidence from the text to answer questions
- Work out the meaning of new words

Language tip
Shusha Guppy's use of the phrase 'the poor' is a good example of how an adjective can be used as a **mass noun** to define a group of people by what they have in common. Other examples include: 'the rich' and 'the fortunate'.

- Work out the meaning of proverbs
- Write lines for a poem
- Work out the meaning of new words

Healthy living

Read these proverbs about being healthy. What do they mean? Do you agree with them?

- 'An apple a day keeps the doctor away.'
- 'Early to bed, early to rise, keeps a person healthy, wealthy and wise.'
- 'Prevention is better than cure.'
- 'You are what you eat.'

Now read this poem about a healthy lifestyle. Copy the poem, adding five more lines before the last line. Use the 'Language tip' on this page to check you are using 'less' and 'fewer' correctly!

If you have...

Fewer fizzy drinks, more clean water

    Fewer sugary snacks, more fresh fruit

Fewer meat products, more leafy vegetables

    Less being driven, more going on foot

Fewer worrying thoughts, more cheerful laughter

    Less internet surfing, more early nights ...

Then you will have a healthy lifestyle.

> **Language tip**
>
> The words '**less**' and '**fewer**' are often confused in English.
>
> We use 'less' with **uncountable nouns** (nouns without a plural form).
>
> For example: 'I listen to <u>less</u> music than my sister.' ('Music' does not have a plural form.)
>
> We use 'fewer' with **countable nouns** (nouns with a plural form).
>
> For example: 'I have <u>fewer</u> books than my brother.' ('Books' is the plural form of 'book'.)

Here's a quick quiz about healthy living. Answer the questions and see if you know what's really good for you.

1. Which of the following lowers levels of stress hormones and strengthens the immune system?

   A Laughter   **B** Taking naps   **C** Reading   **D** Singing

2. How many essential vitamins does your body need to stay healthy?

   A 11   **B** 19   **C** 13   **D** 17

3. Which of the following foods does NOT contain vitamin C?

   A Kiwi   **B** Salmon   **C** Tomatoes   **D** Eggs

4. Which of the following are superfoods?

   A Blueberries   **B** Whole grains   **C** Avocados   **D** All of these

5. How many hours of sleep does an average teenager need?

   A 7–8   **B** 11–13   **C** 8–10   **D** 6–7

- Discuss quiz answers
- Write quiz questions

6 How much water should you drink each day?

    A 2.7–3.7 litres   **B** 3 glasses   **C** 2.5 litres   **D** 1–2 litres

7 What is calcium good for?

    A Brain power   **B** Skin   **C** Bones   **D** Blood

8 How much exercise should you do every day?

    A At least 1 hour   **B** At least 10 minutes

    C At least 20 minutes   **D** At least half an hour

9 What does aerobic exercise immediately increase?

    A Heart rate   **B** Flexibility

    C Muscle tightness   **D** Mobility

10 If everybody reduced the amount of meat in their diets, what else would be reduced?

    A Greenhouse gas emissions   **B** Forest destruction

    C Risk of cancer and heart disease   **D** Soil and water pollution

Your teacher will give you the answers.

8–10 correct answers	**5–7 correct answers**	**3–4 correct answers**	**0–2 correct answers**
Wow, you're a health expert and really know your stuff! Staying healthy is obviously one of your priorities in life.	You know what's what and how to live a healthy lifestyle. You're aware of what's good for you and what's not, and usually make healthy choices.	Well perhaps you're a bit rusty in some areas, but it seems you know some things about the healthy options in life.	Hmm, it might be a good idea to do a little more research about your healthy options. It might not be so critical now, but it's best to get into good habits early on!

 Stretch zone

Write some more multiple-choice questions on health and diet.
Think about facts you know from other school subjects.

Treatments for boils, aches and fevers

Lila, a young girl from a poor village family, is desperate to get help for her very sick mother. In this extract, Lila sits waiting for the arrival of the village medicine man with her younger sisters, Bela and Kamal.

The medicine man's visit

There was nothing to do but wait. At last Lila and her sisters heard the throbbing of the drum and the long eerie blasts on the trumpet. The medicine man was near! He was preceded by the little cow

5   that he dressed in necklaces of beads and an embroidered cloth. [...] He was a sharp-looking man and he kept all kinds of powders and pills in packets tied into the folds of his white clothes. With these he treated the villagers for their

10 boils, aches and fevers. [...] All this gave him the air of a magician which made the girls shiver slightly when they heard him approach. He raised his hand in the air and gave another long blast on his trumpet.

Lila came running out of the house and spoke to

15 the man.

"My mother is ill. She has been ill for a long time. Now she has fever too. Have you any medicine for fever? Have you any medicine for making her strong? She is so weak," Lila explained.

20 "Slowly, slowly, daughter. What is the hurry? First I must have water for my cow – fresh well water. Next, I must have grass for her. Fresh, tender grass. Then I will come and see your mother."

So that was how things had to be done. After the cow had

25 been looked after, he too demanded attention. Lila had to give him tea which he sipped, sitting down under the frangipani tree while the girls stood before him and told him how their mother was growing weaker and weaker. She was refusing to eat and was unable to get up at all.

A treasured cow wearing a garland

Glossary

throbbing beating or sounding with a strong, regular rhythm
eerie strange and frightening
fevers abnormally high body temperatures

- Read and enjoy fiction set in a different time and culture
- Use implicit and explicit evidence from the text to answer questions
- Explain how character is developed

Comprehension

1 Why didn't the medicine man go and see the children's mother straightaway?

1 How does the writer make the medicine man's entrance very theatrical?

1 What kind of regard do you think the medicine man has for the cow, the girl's mother and for himself?

2 What does the medicine man's attitude towards Lila's sense of urgency show about him?

3 What do you think the writer meant by 'a sharp-looking man'? (lines 6–7)

The medicine man's visit (*continued*)

"And now she is hot with fever," Lila wailed suddenly, no longer able to speak calmly.

The man looked at her with his sharp, bright eyes. He got up quickly and started being very busy. To their surprise he did not
5   go in to see their mother as they had expected he would. Instead, he ordered them to build a fire. He wanted a particular kind of wood and the sticks had to be laid just so. Once the fire had started crackling, he flung in packets of flowers that he took from a bag on the cow's back – jasmine, marigold, hibiscus and
10 frangipani. [...] When the fire had died down, he poked at it with a long stick, scattering the ashes so that they cooled.

Jasmine, frangipani, hibiscus and marigold flowers

- Read and enjoy fiction set in a different time and culture
- Use implicit and explicit evidence from the text to answer questions
- Explain how character is developed

Then he scooped them up into his hand and asked for water. He poured a little into the palm of his hand and with one thumb and forefinger he mixed it with the ash. Then he went
15 in to see their mother at last.

She was lying on her side with her eyes closed. When he spoke to her, she turned over and opened her eyes in fear. Lila put her hand on her mother's forehead and spoke to her soothingly. The man told her to open her mouth and put out her tongue
20 which she did, and on it he dropped some of the ash. "Eat, sister," he said. " [...] ash will purify you within. It will drive away the demons that create the fever. Swallow." He kept rolling small balls of ash between his fingers and dropping them into her mouth, making her swallow them. Then he
25 clapped his hands together and walked out.

Glossary

crackling making a rapid succession of short sharp noises
soothingly having a gently calming effect
purify make pure, cleanse something

Comprehension

A

1 What finally makes the medicine man start creating the mother's medicine?
2 Explain how the medicine man makes the little balls of ash which he gives to the children's mother.

B

1 What do Lila's words and the word 'wailed' tell you about how she was feeling? (line 1)
2 The medicine man wanted a 'particular kind of wood' and the children had to lay the sticks 'just so'. What do these phrases tell you about the medicine man?

C

1 How do you think the mother will react to eating ash?

The medicine man's visit (*continued*)

The girls followed, dazed.

"Sweep up all that ash. Collect it. Bring it to me," he ordered, and they obeyed. He pulled some leaves out of his bag and made them put the ash on the leaves, then rolled them up and
5 tied them into neat packets with bits of thread. [...] "Here," he said, handing them to the girls. "Go and put one packet under her pillow. It will drive away the fever-demon. Go and put the others under your own pillows. It will keep you safe from the demons. I have blessed it." He blew on his trumpet.

- Read and enjoy fiction set in a different time and culture
- Use implicit and explicit evidence from the text to answer questions
- Explain how character is developed

10   He then stared down into their faces and looked very fierce. "So?" he shouted at them. [...] Got nothing to give me but your stares? Think I can fill my stomach with your stares? Think I do it all for free?"

Lila ran into the hut. Bela and Kamal stared after her knowing
15   there was no money. But she came out with something in her hand and when she handed it over the girls saw what it was – the ring their mother used to wear when she was well [...] The girls gave a little gasp of astonishment but the man merely snatched it out of Lila's hand, stared at it and then at them.
20   He tucked it away and marched off towards his cow without a word of thanks. [...]

The girls were left staring at the leaf-packets in their hands. "What shall we do with them?" Bela and Kamal asked. Lila clutched the one in her hand as if she wanted to tear it apart.
25   "What *can* we do?" she cried. "We can't do anything – we have to listen to him. [...] We have no one but the man to help us," she said fiercely and marched into the hut to do what the man had told her to.

From *The Village by the Sea*

Comprehension

1 How were the packets of ash to be used, according to the medicine man's instructions?

2 What were the children doing when the medicine man said, "Got nothing to give me but your stares"? What did he want?

3 What did Lila give the medicine man? Why do you think she gave him this?

B

1 What do we find out about the medicine man's character? Use specific adjectives, verbs and phrases from the extract to explain your answer.

2 Why is the medicine man's metaphor about not being able to "fill my stomach with your stares" effective? (lines 11–13)

3 How did Lila feel about the whole situation after the medicine man had gone? Find quotations in the text to support your answer.

C

1 Do you think the medicine man's remedy will help Lila's mother get better? Why?/Why not?

2 What kind of man do you think the medicine man is? Select evidence from the text to support your answer.

Write a letter

Imagine that you are Lila. Your aunt knows that your mother is ill and she is anxious to know how her sister is. Write a letter to your aunt and tell her all about the visit of the medicine man.

- Describe the situation at home and your mother's illness.
- Describe the visit from the medicine man and include your feelings about how he behaved.
- Tell your aunt whether or not you have confidence in his treatment.

You may use the words in the green box on the right to help you.

Judge a book by its cover

When choosing a book, it's often the cover that makes you want to read it. What would you put on the cover of *The Village by the Sea,* based on the extract you just read? Discuss in small groups.

Based on the covers below, which of the books would you like to read? Why? Which books would you not like to read? Why not?

Choose one of the covers and write some information to go on the back of the book. The blurb is the most important thing on the back cover as it summarizes the book. It should tell the reader enough to entice them to read it, but shouldn't explain the whole plot. Make up the story and describe it in powerful language to entice the reader. Your back cover information should include the following details:

- book summary (the 'blurb')
- quotation from a reviewer/reader
- details of the publisher
- price details.

- Select formal or informal registers and vocabulary which are appropriate for the purpose and audience
- Know when to use Standard English and Non-Standard English
- Write from a particular point of view
- Look at and discuss a book cover
- Discuss a topic using specialized vocabulary

helpless   frustrated
desperate   responsible
anxious   traditional
to trust   to demand
to take advantage of
business   benefit   beneficial

5 New pastures

What is it like to start a new life in another country?

> 'Tomorrow to fresh woods and pastures new'
>
> From 'Lycidas' by JOHN MILTON

Talk about ...

- If you and your family had to go and live in a country on the other side of the world, what do you think you would miss most of all about where you live now?
- What things (clothes, attitudes, food) are unique to your country that you would be sad to leave behind?
- Is there anything you would be happy to see changed?

Word origins

nostalgia (n), from the Greek word *nostos*, meaning 'return home' and *algos*, meaning 'pain'. The suffix *-algia* is used a lot in medical terminology.
Related words:
- myalgia (muscle pain)
- cephalgia (headache)

The English poet Milton uses the phrase 'fresh woods and pastures new' as a metaphor for a new start in life. A pasture is a place where animals such as cows or sheep graze. Some people choose to uproot their lives to make a new start in another country. Others are forced to move due to circumstances such as war or famine.

Is moving to new pastures something you or someone in your family has ever experienced? Did you or they experience any homesickness, or nostalgia?

- Read the development of ideas in an informal letter
- Identify the features of informal letters
- Write an informal letter

The start of a new adventure

Read the letter below. It is from a young teacher from the UK who has made a fresh start in Žilina, Slovakia. She has a new job teaching English to adult students, and she is writing to update her friend Sarah.

Dear Sarah,   22 January

Wow, can you believe I've been here three weeks already?! You never thought I'd do it, did you, but here I am – and I've already made loads of new friends. It was an eventful journey. As we drove off the ferry at 5.30 am, Dan suddenly asked me which way to go, which was a bit of a shock! He had
5   shown me the route on the map on the ferry the night before, just before we turned in for the night. I thought he was just being chummy – I didn't realize he wanted me to navigate! Just as well his satnav is up to date!

Anyway, we arrived in Žilina at lunchtime and had to get ready to teach immediately as our first classes started in the afternoon. I have three classes
10   and I've made friends in each class. The students made me feel so welcome and have already invited me into their homes to try their local grub and have taken me on trips to see …

Comprehension

1 Where has the letter writer gone? Why?
2 How are the young teachers travelling?

1 This is an informal letter to a friend. Find examples of language features which are typical of informal writing.
2 What punctuation features also show that the letter is informal?
3 In the letter, the writer uses some colloquial language. What do you think the following mean: 'turned in', 'up to date', 'being chummy', 'grub'?

1 Imagine a teacher from the UK came to your country and you wanted to show them everything that is best about your culture and your area. Where would you take them? What would you do with them? What food and drink would you introduce them to?
2 What other ways can we help people from other countries to feel welcome in a new place?

Finish the letter

Imagine you are the teacher from the UK who has written the letter. The students have done all the things you suggested in question C1 to show you how wonderful their region is. Complete the letter to your friend back home, describing what you have done. Remember to use the same informal tone and other features of informal writing.

- Read and enjoy autobiography set in a different time and culture
- Explore how setting and character are developed

Making a new home

In this extract from her autobiography, Ghada Karmi describes her arrival in London. She was seven years old when she arrived with her mother, brother and sister. They came to join Ghada's father, who was already working in London. The family had to leave their home in Jerusalem when it became too dangerous to stay there in 1948. They fled to safety to Ghada's grandparents in Damascus in Syria before travelling on to London.

Arriving in London

London looked like nothing that I had ever seen. Neither Jerusalem nor Damascus had prepared me for this cold northern city. In fact, the weather was fine and sunny and, although we did not know it then, quite mild for the time of year. My sister
5 said, "Why isn't it raining? They said it always rained in London." I remember thinking when we were in the taxi driving towards our house that all the cars were driving on the wrong side of the road. And how green everything was! I had never seen such greenness in my life. The garden of our house in
10 Jerusalem had its varied trees, its vine and flowers, but the colours of everything there were muted by contrast to the rich greenness of England. I was overwhelmed by the strangeness.

Our house was one of a row of almost identical houses stuck to each other on both sides, 'terraced', the English called it, and
15 nothing like our 'detached' house in Jerusalem. In front, it had a wooden gate and a hedge which acted like a wall. Beyond this was the front door with the number 133 on it and a small window with a frosted glass pane to the side. Inside, it was dark and cold and there were stairs leading to the upper floor.
20 Downstairs, there were two rooms, a kitchen and a scullery.

My mother had been accustomed to our stone villa with its tiled floors and open veranda, and this cramped house with its wooden floorboards and small rooms did not appeal to her. The door of the scullery at the back of the house opened onto
25 the back garden, which was long and narrow and bordered on both sides by wooden fences. It was overgrown with a mass of weeds and long grass out of which struggled two mature apple trees against the end wall. Backing onto the scullery wall was an outside toilet, which was not now in use. Its door was

Glossary

mild warm
muted quieter and softer; less vibrant
overwhelmed had a strong emotional effect on
scullery small room next to the kitchen in an old house, originally used for washing dishes

70

30 barely hanging on its hinges and we started to use it as a place to put junk of all sorts.

I try to remember now when I first saw our new home in London. Did I look at that dreary suburban street with its small, dark houses, all standing in monotonous rows and
35 compare it to what I had known in Jerusalem? Did I feel the stark contrast between the two and grieve for what had been lost? I don't think I did, because I had by then already closed off the Palestine of my childhood into a private memory place where it would always remain magically frozen in time. My
40 mother, on the other hand, had decided to recreate Palestine in London.

She started first with the floors. In the Arab world floors are usually made of stone or tiles because of the hot summers. Housewives, or their servants if they had them, washed the
45 floors regularly to clean them but also to keep the houses cool. In no time, and despite England's cold weather, my mother removed the carpets which covered the kitchen and the hall and had the floor laid with reddish brown, shiny tiles to simulate our house in Jerusalem. She would fill a bucket with soap and
50 water and slosh it all over the floor, get down on her knees and mop it up vigorously with a cloth.

Upstairs there were no carpets and the floor was covered in linoleum. This was in the days before central heating, and on some winter mornings it was so cold that our bedroom windows
55 were covered with a layer of frost on the inside. Likewise, the linoleum on the floor was ice-cold to the touch of our warm feet. So we would curl our feet over onto their sides to minimize contact with the floor and hobble over to get our slippers.

From *In Search of Fatima: A Palestinian Story* by GHADA KARMI

Ice on the window panes

- Read and enjoy autobiography set in a different time and culture
- Work out the meaning of new words
- Explore how setting and character are developed

Glossary

accustomed to used to thinking something is normal or natural having experienced it regularly over a period of time

junk old or discarded articles that are considered useless or of little value

monotonous boring and repetitious

simulate copy the appearance or character of something

Word origins

minimize (v), from the Latin word *minimus*, meaning 'smallest' or 'least'
Related words:
- minimal
- minimum

Language tip
When you look up a verb in the dictionary, you will find it in the **infinitive** form. This is the basic form of the verb without any subject or tense. It will sometimes have the word 'to' in front of it. If you wanted to look up 'minimizing', 'minimized', or 'minimizes', for example, you would always find the infinitive 'minimize' listed in the dictionary.

- Use implicit and explicit evidence from the text to answer questions
- Understand how texts reflect when and where they were written

Comprehension

1 As the writer sits in the taxi, what two features of London surprise her the most?

2 Why are the words 'terraced' and 'detached' in inverted commas?

3 Explain why it is impractical to have tiled flooring in the London house rather than carpets.

4 Why is the mother so insistent on tiles rather than carpets?

1 In paragraph 2, what effect does the writer create by using the word 'stuck' to describe terraced houses?

2 In paragraph 3, what effect does the writer create by using the word 'struggled' to describe the apple trees?

1 What makes the London home feel so confined to the writer?

2 Why do you think it is harder for the writer's mother to adjust to London than it is for the writer?

3 Copy and complete the table below, outlining the differences between the two houses.

	London	Jerusalem
Colours of foliage		
Type of house		
Exterior of house		
Rooms		
Flooring		
Back garden		

?

Ghada's mother took up the carpets and replaced the flooring with tiles to make her London house feel more like home. If you moved to another country, what would you do to make the house you live in feel more like home? Is it important to you that home reminds you of where you come from? Why? Why not?

Stretch zone

Imagine you are Ghada. You have been in London for one month. Write a letter to your best friend back in Jerusalem telling them all about London and your new home.

- Discuss similarities and differences in photographs
- Discuss a topic using accurate linguistic terminology

Compare two places

Compare and contrast the different types of houses and streets that Ghada experienced in Jerusalem and London. Use the photographs below and re-read Ghada's descriptions on pages 70–71. As you write, try using 'neither … nor' and 'either … or'.

- What are the main differences between the two places?
- What do you think the family would find most difficult to adapt to?
- What advice would you give to Ghada in her new home in London?
- Which city would you rather live in? Why?

Language tip

'Neither … nor' connects two or more negative alternatives.

For example: 'Neither Jerusalem nor Damascus was anything like London.'

'Either … or' connects two or more positive alternatives.

For example: 'I could live in either Jerusalem or London.'

This is what traditional housing looked like in Jerusalem in 1948.

This is what traditional housing looked like in London in 1948.

Write a comparison

Write a comparison between two places that you have lived in. It could be two houses in different countries; two houses in the same country but different cities, towns or villages; or two different houses in the same city, town or village. Perhaps you moved to a new part of town or from an apartment to a house with a garden. If you have lived in the same house all your life, make a comparison with another house you know well. It could be a friend's house or a relative's house. Imagine what it would be like to move to that house.

- Describe the similarities and differences between the two places.
- How did moving house change your life? In what ways did it stay the same?
- If possible, find photographs to go with your description.

When you have finished writing, swap your comparison with a partner. Proofread your partner's comparison for any errors in punctuation, grammar or spelling. Say what you liked about the comparison and make a suggestion for how your partner can improve their writing.

Write out a final version of your comparison and, if you can, add pictures. Make a classroom display of your work.

> - Write a comparison of two places, using appropriate style, structure and vocabulary
> - Proofread text and suggest improvements

Do any of these homes look like yours?

Life of a refugee

The poet Rashid Hussein was born in 1936 in a village near Haifa in Palestine. Later, he moved to New York. One of his most famous poems describes the sadness of a displaced person, living in a refugee camp and dreaming of the place where he grew up. Below is an extract from this poem.

- Read and enjoy poetry set in a different time and culture
- Work out the meaning of new words
- Discuss how poets play with themes and conventions
- Communicate personal opinions confidently

from Tent #50 (Song of a Refugee)

Tent #50, on the left, that is my present,
But it is too cramped to contain a future.
And "Forget!": they say, but how can I?
   Teach the night to forget to bring
5   Dreams showing me my village
   And teach the wind to forget to carry to me
The aroma of apricots in my fields!
   And teach the sky, too, to forget to rain.
Only then may I forget my country.

RASHID HUSSEIN

Glossary

displaced someone who is forced to leave their homeland and has no country of residence

refugee person who has to leave their country in order to escape war, persecution or natural disaster

Talk about …

- How does this poem help you think about the conflicting emotions and feelings of a displaced person?
- Do you think it is possible to look forward to a new life while thinking about what you have left behind?
- Discuss the frustrations you might feel if you were living in a refugee camp.
- How important are the senses in holding on to the memory of a place?

Comprehension

A

1 Why does the person in the poem describe 'Tent # 50' as his/her present?

2 Which three things remind the person of their home?

3 Do you think that the person will ever be able to forget his/her country? Give evidence from the poem to support your answer.

B

1 What does the person in the poem mean by 'too crammed to contain a future'?

2 Why is 'forget' in double inverted commas? (line 3) Who does 'they' on the same line refer to?

3 Identify a word in the poem that appeals to the senses.

C

1 What do you think would be the worst thing about living in a refugee camp?

2 What other problems would there be in such a large area of temporary accommodation? Think of sanitation, spread of disease, education, keeping people occupied and any of your own ideas.

3 Why is it sometimes difficult for countries to find suitable accommodation for refugees?

- Use implicit and explicit evidence from the text to answer questions
- Explain how language features create effects
- Participate in active role-play

Imagine you are a refugee

1 You are going to exercise your imagination! Ask a partner to close their eyes and listen to your description of living in a tent in a refugee camp. Imagine you are weaving your way through the other tents to get back to your own. Describe everything you can see (children playing, adults working and talking, livestock, pets ...); hear (laughter, whispering, arguments, animal sounds ...); smell (waste, animals, cooking ...); feel (beneath your feet or as you brush past); taste (on the air). Try to make your description really vivid so your partner can imagine they are there too.

2 Swap roles. This time you close your eyes and listen to your partner's description. They must imagine walking barefooted through an apricot orchard (like the one Rashid Hussein mentions in his poem). They describe what they can see, hear, smell, feel and taste.

- Communicate personal ideas confidently

Voyage on the *Empire Windrush*

The poet John Agard was born in Guyana, the year after the SS *Empire Windrush* brought the first 800 immigrants from Jamaica in the Caribbean to the UK, a journey of 8,000 miles. This historic voyage led the way for the mass immigration of Caribbean people into the UK. Agard made the journey in 1977 and, since arriving in the UK, he has worked to bring Caribbean culture to British audiences.

John Agard dedicated the poem you are about to read to Vince Reid who, at the age of 13, was one of the very youngest passengers on the ship. Before you read the poem, look at the Glossary box on this page to help you to understand it.

Talk about ...

Look at all the people on the *Empire Windrush*. The 8,000-mile journey from the Caribbean to Tilbury Docks in England took 30 days.

Imagine you are on the *Empire Windrush*, part of one of the first groups of Caribbean people to arrive in the UK. What do you think the atmosphere would be like on board the ship? Do you think people would be sad, excited – a mixture of both?

The *Empire Windrush* arriving at Tilbury Docks in London, 1948

Glossary

yard *(West Indian or Caribbean English)* house or home

mango juicy tropical fruit with yellow/orange flesh

walk good walk good *(Caribbean idiom)* walk well and do well

spinning turning or causing to turn or whirl round quickly

beacon light or other visible object serving as a signal, warning or guide

mind-opening willingness to listen to or accept different ideas or opinions

Windrush Child

Behind you
Windrush child
palm trees wave goodbye

above you
5   Windrush child
seabirds asking why

around you
Windrush child
blue water rolling by

10   beside you
Windrush child
your Windrush mum and dad

think of storytime yard
and mango mornings

15   and new beginnings
doors closing and opening

will things turn out right?
At least the ship will arrive
in midsummer light

20   and you Windrush child
think of grandmother
telling you don't forget to write

and with one last hug
walk good walk good
25   and the sea's wheel carries on spinning

and from that place England
you tell her in a letter
of your Windrush adventure

stepping in a big ship
30   not knowing how long the journey
or that you're stepping into history

bringing your Caribbean eye
to another horizon
grandmother's words your shining beacon

35   learning how to fly
the kite of your dreams
in an English sky

Windrush child
walking good walking good
40   in a mind-opening
meeting of snow and sun

JOHN AGARD

- Use implicit and explicit evidence from a text to answer questions
- Read a poem aloud using verbal and non-verbal techniques
- Write a poem, using a range of sentence features

Comprehension

1 Which lines give you the thoughts of the child's mother and father?
2 What is meant by 'doors closing and opening'?
3 Who is the person that links both worlds in the life of the Windrush child? How will he keep this communication going?
4 How does the poet make clear that this voyage is a significant event in the child's life?
5 Which stanzas look back to life in Jamaica and which ones point ahead to what the Windrush child will experience in England?

1 Give two examples of personification from lines 1–9.
2 In the poem, the writer starts some stanzas with a prepositional phrase, which gives a particular emphasis. Compare lines 10–12 with the sentence 'Your Windrush mum and dad sit beside you Windrush child.' Which is most effective? Why?
3 What does 'the sea's wheel' refer to? (line 25)

1 What do you think could be the 'mango mornings' that the child's parents remember? (line 14)
2 In what way are the words of the child's grandmother a 'shining beacon'? (line 34)
3 Explain the final two lines of the poem. Which two countries are meeting and in what way is the meeting 'mind-opening'? What do you think will happen next for the Windrush child?

Perform the poem

Practise reading the poem out loud. Read it with a partner or take turns to read stanzas. Emphasize the prepositional phrases with exaggerated arm movements. For example, stand looking forward but point behind you when reciting the beginning of the poem. Perform your recital for another pair.

Write a poem

Write a poem similar to 'Windrush Child'. Imagine you are leaving your country to live in another country, which is very different from your own. You are not travelling by boat but a different form of transport.

- Decide which country you are moving to (hot, cold, wet, dry, flat, hilly, populous, empty, built-up, or your own ideas).
- Decide on the type of transport (plane, train, car, bicycle, horse and cart, flying carpet, or your own idea).
- Use prepositional phrases to describe what you will be leaving behind in your country, what you can see as you travel and what is ahead in your new life in the new country.

Language tip

The poem 'Windrush Child' uses various **prepositions** that describe the relative placement of things: 'behind you'; 'above you'; 'around you'; 'beside you'.

They are usually used after a verb.

For example:

'I <u>sit behind</u> Sally in my History class.'

'The bird <u>flew high</u> above me in the sky.'

Coming to Britain

All the young people featured here came to Britain to start a new life at some point in their lives. They came from many different parts of the world for a range of reasons. The interview clips that follow express their feelings and experiences.

- Read and enjoy autobiography
- Work out the meaning of new words
- Understand how a point of view can be conveyed in different texts

I was a baby when I left Guatemala. When I was born my actual parents already had six other children and couldn't look after me as well, so I went to an orphanage. My parents were looking for another child to adopt, and they saw a picture of me. They brought me to the UK and welcomed me home. Sometimes I think about my brothers and sisters in Guatemala and what life would have been like there. I would probably be working in the fields. I love my life here. It's the only life I know. I feel British. This is my home – where Mum and Dad and all my friends are. Maybe when I'm older, I will visit Guatemala.

Ada, aged 9

Inza, aged 15

When my parents told me, Inza, we're moving to England, I thought it was going to be paradise. But when we left the airport and went to our new home I couldn't believe how cold and dark it was. In South Sudan, you get kids everywhere and it's not hard to make friends. In England, there's no one around. You've always got to be careful. I have to phone my mum and tell her where I am and what I'm doing so that she knows I'm safe. I miss the free life in South Sudan. There's too much crime here. I feel happy to be with my parents but I don't feel at home in England. When I'm older and have made some money, I will go back to South Sudan and build a big house for all my family to live in.

Glossary

orphanage residential place for the care and education of children

adopt legally bring up someone else's child as one's own

- Read and enjoy autobiography
- Work out the meaning of new words
- Understand how a point of view can be conveyed in different texts

During the summer, I turned 13. I should have been happy but I felt miserable. My mother, my little brother and I had just arrived in London from Afghanistan. We were moved into a hostel in the affluent northwest of the city. The journey to London had been difficult and challenging, and we were forced to separate from my father and older brother a few weeks earlier. The hostel was situated on a beautiful tree-lined avenue. A pleasant walk north took you to Hampstead Heath and to the south was Regent's Park. Every day, we would walk around and around the park's ornate rose garden and then sit by the fountain – our favourite spot – waiting for any news about my father and brother. I missed them terribly and didn't understand why we had been forced to split up. It took six months before we were reunited with them. Now we're all together and that's all that matters.

Teena, aged 15

I live in council housing with my brother and parents. We emigrated here five years ago when I was nine. My family doesn't have much money, but my parents make school a priority. I picked up English really quickly. My dad was a civil engineer back home and is brilliant at maths so he helps me a lot. When I started school and made friends, I finally got to see how British people live (not just the stereotypes!) – what they really do, eat and talk about. My biggest challenge so far has been coping with feeling different to everyone else. I can't really invite my friends back to my house for a sleepover or girl's night. My parents have different cultural expectations to my friends' parents. They haven't really integrated as well as my brother and me. It's easy for us because we can meet friends at school. Mum and Dad are more isolated.

Hae Won, aged 15

Glossary

affluent rich, wealthy
integrated mixed in with others
isolated alone, away from others
stereotype widely held but oversimplified image or idea of a particular type of person or thing
council housing *(British)* houses owned by the local administration and rented to tenants

Word origins

stereotype (n), from the French adjective *stéréotype*, which comes from the Greek word *stereos*, meaning 'solid, firm' and *typos*, meaning 'impression'
Related words:
- archetype
- prototype

- Use implicit and explicit evidence from a text to answer questions
- Communicate personal opinons confidently

Comprehension

1 Which child …

  a used to go for long walks in the park with family?

  b feels their parents have had more problems settling in the UK than them?

  c can't remember anything about the country they were born in?

  d felt the trauma of family separation?

  e is expected to work very hard at school?

  f thinks of the UK as her mother country?

  g was initially very excited about coming to the UK?

  h is worried about safety on the streets in the UK?

1 Answer the following questions by explaining how you know and giving evidence from the text to support your opinion.

Which child …

  a is completely disillusioned with the UK?

  b is the least affected by their move to the UK?

  c thinks that nothing is as important as the family being united?

  d feels slightly embarrassed by their parents' attitude?

1 Who do you think has the most difficulties adjusting to the lifestyle of another country – the parents or children? Why? Do you think it gets easier over time? What about the next generation? Do you think they will still have any attachment to the country where one or more of their parents and grandparents came from?

2 What problems do you think someone from another country might have if they came to live in your country? For example, are there any traditions or national habits they would need to get used to?

Talk about …

- What do you think might be the best ways of coping with life in a new country?
- Do you think it's important for people to remember where they have come from and maintain their cultural identity?

Writing a response

Read Maher's interview below. Write an email to him asking questions or offering advice. Tell him about your life and try to find things in his account that you both share (for example, caring about education or going out with friends).

- Communicate personal opinions confidently
- Select formal or informal registers and vocabulary which are appropriate for the purpose and audience
- Proofread and edit writing

I used to live in Damascus, but it wasn't safe. I was walking to school one morning and heard an airstrike – a bomb fell in front of me. I was on my own and I thought, "It's going to end here." I was 15 years old when we moved to Britain and I found the transition really hard. My life in Syria was normal. I was just a typical teenager going out every weekend with my friends. And that's what I expected coming here, but things didn't turn out that way. The biggest struggle was the language barrier. I didn't know any English so I had a lot of trouble getting into school. It was horrible because I really care about education. I had stereotypical expectations of the UK. I thought we were going to be welcomed by our friendly neighbours, but that didn't happen. Our neighbours never knock on the door, but I guess it's just a different lifestyle. I'm used to it now and I like it. This is my life now.

Maher, aged 16

An interview

Choose a person you admire and ask if you can interview them. Talk to them about their experiences of change and new starts in life. Ask questions about their feelings as well as facts. Perhaps they have some dramatic or funny stories to tell. Jot down notes as they speak.

Now select the best material from your notes and write them up as a transcript of an interview clip.

Your future

Think and write about what you want to do with your life: where you want to live, what your house would be like, who you would live with, what career you would pursue, and what hobbies and interests you would have. There are no limits to this – you can be an astronaut, a writer, a scientist, a famous actor, or anyone you like. Remember that you are now a grown-up and the world may have changed in many different ways. Enjoy exploring your future!

What makes a good beginning?

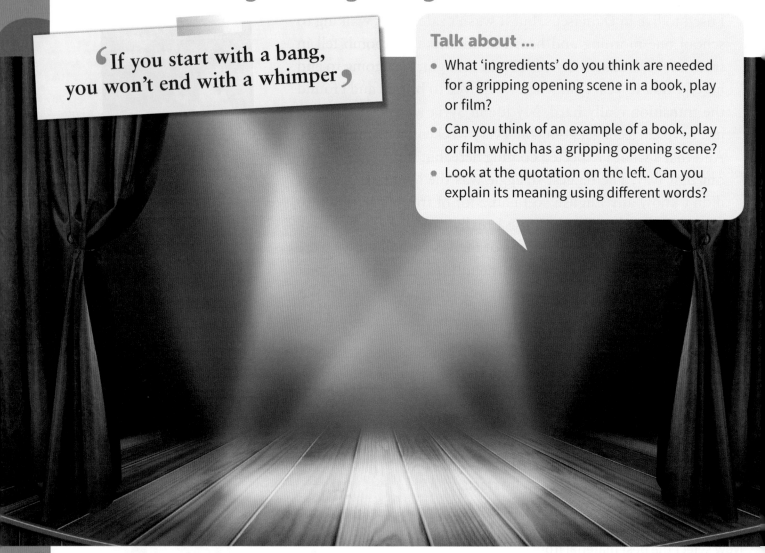

'If you start with a bang, you won't end with a whimper'

Talk about ...

- What 'ingredients' do you think are needed for a gripping opening scene in a book, play or film?
- Can you think of an example of a book, play or film which has a gripping opening scene?
- Look at the quotation on the left. Can you explain its meaning using different words?

Charles Dickens (1812–1870) is one of the greatest English novelists. Many of his novels have been made into films, plays and musicals.

Great Expectations was first published in an illustrated magazine, with one or two chapters appearing each week, so it needed to be written in a way that kept readers interested. The opening pages of *Great Expectations* are the most dramatic of all Dickens's novels, and one of the most terrifying and atmospheric starts to a story in all of literature.

At the start of this unit, you will be reading, acting and writing a playscript version of the story.

Great Expectations

Time   *Christmas Eve, 1812*

Place   *The Kent marshes, a bleak stretch of wind-swept, empty land on the south side of the estuary of the River Thames, east of London. Out on the river are the prison hulks. Pip is in the churchyard beside the gravestone of his parents and his baby brothers.*

Cast of Characters

Pip   *Ten-year-old Pip is an orphan. He lives with his sister, and her husband, the blacksmith Joe Gargery, in a village a mile from the churchyard.*

Magwitch   *Magwitch is a convict who, in the opening scene, has just escaped from a prison hulk on the Thames, and is still wearing the shackles and leg irons.*

- Read and enjoy a playscript set in a different time and culture
- Explore how setting and character are developed
- Work out the meaning of new words

Learning tip
While you are reading, imagine you are watching this play. Pay attention to the setting and the stage directions.

Act 1

In the Churchyard

Pip   *(Gently moving his hand over the inscription on the gravestone.)*

'Philip Pirrip'. I never even saw you, Father. All I have of you is my name. Philip Pirrip. But Philip Pirrip is so difficult to say. Pip is much easier. 'Also Georgiana Wife of the Above'. That's you, Mother. I wish I could remember you, but I was too young.

5

(The wind whistles through the trees.) And all my little brothers.

10   *(He looks sadly at the five little stones at the base of the gravestone.)* If only they had all lived, I wouldn't have to live now with Mrs Joe. Even though she's my sister, I'm awfully afraid of her rages.

(The wind whistles again. Pip is suddenly afraid.)
15   What's that? *(Trying to comfort himself, but beginning to cry.)* It's only the wind in the reeds.

Glossary

hulk old warship, sometimes used as prisons
blacksmith someone who makes and repairs metal objects
convict someone who has been found guilty of a crime
shackles metal rings connected by a chain, attached to a convict's legs to prevent escape

- Read and enjoy a playscript set in a different time and culture

Magwitch *(Suddenly rising from behind a gravestone, in a terrible voice.)* Hold your noise! Keep still, you little devil, or I'll cut your throat! *(The man has a convict's iron shackle on his leg. He's wet, muddy and badly scratched. He seizes hold of Pip's chin.)*

20

Pip *(terrified)* Oh, don't cut my throat, sir! Please, don't do it sir!

Magwitch Tell us your name! Quick, quick, boy!

25 **Pip** *(stuttering in a whisper)* P-p-p-p-p-Pip, sir.

Magwitch Once again, boy. Speak up, boy!

Pip *(a little louder)* Pip, sir.

Magwitch Show us where you live. Point out the place!

Learning tip

Stage directions appear in brackets and in italics to make it clear that they are not spoken lines.

30

Pip *(pointing to the village a mile away)* There, sir, in the village.

Magwitch *(Suddenly shaking Pip violently and rifling through the pockets of his little jacket. Finding a crust of bread, he eats ravenously. He pushes his face into Pip's as he gnaws the bread.)* You young dog, what fat cheeks you've got! I could eat them!

35

(He puts his rough hands towards Pip's face and Pip flinches.) I could eat them NOW! *(He glares threateningly at Pip.)*

Pip Oh, please don't, sir, please don't think of doing that!

40

Magwitch *(grinning slightly and patting Pip on the cheek)* Now, boy, where's your mother?

Pip There, sir. *(The man jumps with sudden fear and starts to run.)* There, sir. 'Also Georgiana Wife of the Above'. That's my mother.

45

Magwitch Oh! *(returns to Pip's side)* Oh, so that's your mother. And that's your father alongside?

Pip Yes, sir, that's him.

Magwitch Huh! So who do you live with? That is supposing that I let you live – which I haven't made up my mind about yet.

50

Pip *(shivering)* Oh, let me live, sir. I live with my sister, Mrs Joe, sir. Wife of Mr Joe Gargery, the blacksmith.

Magwitch *(his eyes widen)* Blacksmith, eh?

55

(He looks down at the iron on his leg. He seems to be thinking deeply.) Blacksmith? Blacksmith, eh?

(He suddenly puts his hands on Pip's shoulders and tilts him backwards.) Now the question is whether you are going to be allowed to live. You know what a file is?

60

Glossary

rifling quickly searching through something
ravenously very hungrily
gnaws keeps biting on something
file tool used to shape or cut metal

- Read and enjoy a playscript set in a different time and culture
- Work out the meaning of new words

Pip *(seriously afraid but too frightened to move)* Yes, sir, I know what a file is.

Magwitch And you know what vittles is? *(He tilts Pip a little more.)*

65 **Pip** Yes, sir, I know what vittles is.

Magwitch *(tilting Pip a little more)* You get me a file! *(He tilts Pip a little more still.)* And you bring me vittles! *(He tilts Pip a little more.)* You bring them both to me, *(tilting him again)* or I'll have your heart and
70 liver out!

Pip *(feeling both sick and frightened)* Please, sir, put me upright and I'll attend to you better.

Magwitch *(standing Pip upright and staring right into his face)* Bring me early tomorrow morning that file and
75 those vittles to that old fort. You do it, and you never dare say a word to anyone, or dare make any sign to anyone that you have ever met such a person as me – and you shall be allowed to live.

Pip *(shivering with cold and fear)* Yes, sir.

80 **Magwitch** But if you don't do as I say, your heart and your liver shall be torn out! Now, I'm not alone as you might think. There's a young man hiding with me and, in comparison with him, I am the gentlest person you could hope to meet. This young man
85 has a special way of getting the heart and liver out of a boy. A boy will hide in vain from this young man. This young man will creep into a boy in bed when he thinks he's safe, and tear him open. At the moment, I'm stopping this young man from doing
90 that, but if you fail … if you fail, I won't be able to stop him! What do you say?

Pip I'll, I'll get you the file and the vittles, sir. I promise, sir. And I'll bring them to the fort early tomorrow morning. I'll find what bits of food I can, I promise.

A dramatized version of the original novel by CHARLES DICKENS

Glossary

liver large organ of the body that detoxifies the blood

Comprehension

1 Why is Pip in the churchyard?

2 Why do you think Magwitch is 'wet, muddy and badly scratched'? (lines 20–21) Where has he come from?

3 What is a file, and what would Magwitch do with it?

1 Verbs can be used to create an emotional and dramatic effect. Explain the effect of the following verbs in the text: 'comfort' (line 15), 'terrified' (line 22) and 'shivering' (lines 52 and 79).

2 The author uses various language techniques to create dramatic tension. For example, repetition: "Quick, quick, boy!" (line 24) Name other techniques that have been used and write a quotation showing each one.

1 Why does Magwitch jump with sudden fear when Pip points to where his mother is? (line 43)

2 Why do you think Magwitch's eyes 'widen' when Pip says he lives with a blacksmith? (line 54)

3 What different emotions do you think Magwitch experiences throughout the scene?

4 How do you think Pip is feeling as he makes a promise to Magwitch at the end?

> • Use implicit and explicit evidence from a text to answer questions
> • Explain how language features create effects
> • Understand how characters are portrayed by their actions and dialogue

Stretch zone

When you finish reading the playscript, go back and review words you didn't understand. Look up the definitions in a dictionary and add them to your new word list.

Pip and the convict: a still from a BBC TV production

Have a go at performing

Of course, playscripts were written in order to be performed. Work with a partner to prepare a performance of the *Great Expectations* extract, considering carefully:

- the thoughts and emotions of the characters
- who your audience is (members of your class)
- how you will use intonation, pace and volume effectively
- how you will use action to add to the drama of the scene.

Join with another pair and watch each other's performances. What did you think about the decisions the other pair made?

Be a scriptwriter

Scriptwriters sometimes change things about the original story. With a partner, choose a short section from the *Great Expectations* extract and change the characters and setting. Then:

- write a brief description of the setting in time and place, and the cast of characters (see page 85)
- aim to write five or six lines of dialogue for each character
- include clear stage directions.

Practise reading your adapted script aloud. Then swap scripts with another pair. Perform each other's playscripts and share your feedback.

Stretch zone

Imagine you are the director of this play. Share your vision with the cast of how the play will look on stage. Make notes on the following questions and draw pictures to help the cast imagine it all:

- How would you design the stage set?
- What kind of props and objects would you use?
- What kind of lighting and sound effects would help set the scene?

Objectives sidebar:
- Perform a playscript
- Explain how playwrights use speech and non-verbal devices for effect in performance
- Write a playscript
- Write notes appropriately for the intended audience

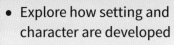

- Explore how setting and character are developed
- Explain how language features create effects
- Communicate personal opinions confidently

How does this poem set the scene?

The following lines are from the famous poem 'The Listeners' by the English poet Walter de la Mare (1873–1956). The poet sets the scene in these opening lines.

The Listeners

'Is there anybody there?' said the Traveller,

    Knocking on the moonlit door;

And his horse in the silence champed the grasses

    Of the forest's ferny floor;

5 And a bird flew up out of the turret,

    Above the Traveller's head:

And he smote upon the door again a second time;

    'Is there anybody there?' he said.

WALTER DE LA MARE

Glossary

champed chewed
ferny covered with ferns (made up word)
smote hit very hard (a very old word, rarely used today)

Comprehension

 A

1 Describe what is happening in the poem.

 B

1 Write one example of each of the following from the poem: alliteration, rhyme, repetition.
2 How do we know it is a lonely, quiet place?
3 How would you describe the atmosphere that the poet creates?

 C

1 What do you think will happen next in the poem? Choose one scenario to share with the class.

Language tip

Examples of poetic devices:
Alliteration – 'silently, sliding snake'
Rhyme – 'the cat sat on the mat'
Repetition – 'Do I want cake? Yes, yes, yes!'

- Explain how language features create effects
- Write a poem, using poetic devices

Let's compare poems

Below is the first stanza from the narrative poem, 'The Walrus and the Carpenter' by Lewis Carroll (1832–1898), which appeared in his book *Alice Through the Looking Glass*. The opening lines set the scene, using contradictory humour and vivid imagery. While reading, consider how the mood and atmosphere contrast with the opening lines of 'The Listeners' on page 91.

The Walrus and the Carpenter

The sun was shining on the sea,

Shining with all his might:

He did his very best to make

The billows smooth and bright –

5 And this was odd, because it was

The middle of the night.

LEWIS CARROLL

Comprehension

1 What poetic devices have been used in 'The Walrus and the Carpenter'? Give examples and name the techniques.

Be a poet

Now it is your turn to be a poet! Write your own short poem or opening stanza for a longer poem.

- Think about how you will capture the reader's attention in your opening lines.
- Consider the mood and atmosphere you wish to create: sombre, humorous, scary, silly, melancholy?
- Use poetic devices to help create effect.

When you are happy with the first draft of your poem, read it to a partner. Ask for feedback and suggestions to improve your poem and then write the final version.

Language tip

Literary techniques make images more powerful in a poem. For example:

Simile – comparing two different things by saying one thing is like another. 'He's like a cat on a hot tin roof.'

Metaphor – comparing two things by saying something is something else (when in fact it is not). 'She's a night owl – she never wants to go to bed.'

Personification – describing inanimate objects as if they are human or have human qualities. 'The wind gently kissed my cheek.'

Stretch zone

Go back to your poem and check if you have included these poetic devices:

- alliteration
- rhyme
- repetition.

Add a new stanza and include simile, metaphor or personification.

- Read fiction set in a different time and culture
- Work out the meaning of new words

A story from Sri Lanka

The following extract from the novel *Reef* starts out in Sri Lanka in the 1960s, where the author, Romesh Gunesekera, grew up. In this extract, we follow the narrator's account of the curious first day when he enters the big house where he is to be a general servant to Mister Salgado.

Glossary

rathmal rhododendron, a red flowering shrub
jasmine climbing plant with heavily scented flowers

Mister Salgado

"Mister Salgado is a real gentleman. You must do whatever he tells you." My uncle pulled my ear. "You understand? Just do it."

5   I was eleven years old. My uncle was escorting me to a house in town I had never been to before. At the base of the two columns at the front of the house were beds of scarlet rathmal and white jasmine. The big windows were shielded by shutters painted in mildewy green. My uncle took me into the back of the house through a side entrance. Inside, a door squeaked
10 behind us, closing automatically. A crumpled old woman was sitting on a small wooden stool with her feet in the sun.

She looked up. "You are back again?" she said to my uncle. "What is all this coming and going?" Her mouth collapsed around her empty gums.

Learning tip

As you read, make notes of words and phrases that tell you about the house and the old woman.

The boy was brought to a house like this in Sri Lanka.

15   My uncle told her we were there to see Mister Salgado. She got up and slowly made her way into the main part of the house.

"I will ask," she mumbled.

We sat on the floor and waited. My ear hurt from my uncle's
20 tug. When the sun sank behind the rooftops, we were summoned by a voice from somewhere deep inside the house. The last rays of light splintered through the trees. My uncle pushed me forward, "Let's go."

At first Mister Salgado said nothing. My uncle too was a man
25 of few words and they were both silent for a while.

Eventually Mister Salgado nodded towards me. "So, this is the boy?"

"Yes, this is the boy." My uncle shifted his weight from one foot to the other.

30 He offered the bag of green mangoes we had brought. "This is the one I was telling about. He is the boy. He can learn very quickly."

A smooth untroubled face stared at me, "School? Did you go?"

"Yes," I blurted out. "I went to school. Fifth Standard. I can
35 read and write." I had even learned some English from my poor schoolmaster who lived in a bungalow near my father's fields.

"And now?"

My uncle wriggled next to me. "As I told before, he can learn quickly but he cannot live at home any more. That
40 trouble …"

Glossary

blurted out said something suddenly without much thought

bungalow house with only one storey

Learning tip
As you read, make notes of words and phrases that tell you about the character of the boy's uncle and Mister Salgado.

?

Consider this 'Mister Salgado' extract. Imagine if, like the boy, you no longer had access to education. How would it impact your life and affect your opportunities?

- Use implicit and explicit evidence from a text to answer questions
- Analyze setting, characters and plot
- Explain how language features create effects

I had burned the thatched roof of a hut in the schoolyard by accident. I only dropped a single match. Blue flame had shot out and caught the thatch. My father went mad; I ran away to my uncle who promised to arrange a new life for me. He
45 told me I would never have to go back again. "I am doing this only because I think your mother – if she were alive – would have wanted me to. Do you understand?" he had said.

Mister Salgado sighed. He spoke slowly. I had never heard language so gently spoken. Ever after when Mister Salgado
50 spoke, I would be captivated.

From *Reef* by Romesh Gunesekera

Glossary

thatched made from straw
captivated to be very interested

Comprehension

A

1 Which words tell you that the old woman does not have any teeth?
2 How do you know that the uncle and the boy had to wait a long time to see Mister Salgado?
3 How do you know that the uncle had visited Mister Salgado previously?
4 Why does the boy not live with his parents?

B

1 Why does the writer say 'A smooth untroubled face stared at me' (line 33) instead of 'Mr Salgado stared at me'?
2 What effect is created by the boy's short sentences in lines 34–35?
3 Why has the writer used an ellipsis (…) on line 40 to finish the sentence?
4 What impression does the description of the old woman make on you?

C

1 The boy's uncle says Mister Salgado is a "real gentleman." What evidence is there in the story that Mister Salgado lives a more privileged life than the uncle?
2 What sort of man does Mister Salgado seem to be?
3 How do you think the boy will get on as Mister Salgado's servant?

When two characters meet ...

Think of two characters you know well. They can be from a book, film, TV show, play or video game.

Choose a scenario for your two characters:

- an interview
- an argument
- a chance meeting.

Decide where and when the characters meet. Make notes on these before you start writing.

Decide who your audience will be, as this may influence the way your characters speak. For example, your audience might be primary children, members of your class, parents/carers or teachers.

Write the meeting between your two characters and make sure you have included:

- a description of your characters
- a description of the setting
- dialogue between the characters
- a backstory (your characters need to talk about events before this one meeting).

When you have finished, swap your writing with a partner, and provide feedback to each other on how effective your scenes were.

Write a review

Review your partner's scene using this structure:

Characters
- Who were they?
- Describe them.
- Did you find them interesting?

Scenario
- Explain the scenario.

Setting
- Where does the action take place?
- Describe the setting.

Review
- Did you enjoy the scene?
- What worked well?
- What improvements could be made?

- Write organized and structured texts for an intended purpose
- Write appropriately for the intended audience

Glossary

scenario imagined event; summary of a plot

Language tip

When you are writing a review, it is good to be able to use expressive vocabulary.
For example:

- for 'interesting', you could say: 'intriguing', 'captivating', 'fascinating', 'absorbing'
- a book you can't put down might be described as a 'compulsive read', 'gripping', 'enthralling'.

Add these words to your vocabulary list and look up their meanings. Find other words to make your writing more exciting and dramatic.

Have you ever been to the theatre?

Talk about ...

- Have you ever been to a theatre to see a play or a performance? Think of the feeling of excitement you had as the curtains opened. Share your memories with the class.
- At the theatre or concert hall, you can see a play or a musical. What other kinds of performances can you see there?

Shadow puppetry

Did you think of puppet shows in your discussion about the stage? Or shadow puppetry? Shadow puppetry is an ancient form of entertainment.

Read about it in the article on the next page.

Shadow puppet characters from Malaysia

- Read non-fiction
- Work out the meaning of new words

What is shadow puppetry?

Shadow puppetry is considered the oldest form of puppetry in the world. It began thousands of years ago in China and India. It is a living folk art in China and Southeast Asia. In China, the shadow plays are often based on folk tales and

5 legends of the past. In Indonesia, the plays are taken from two religious epics where there is often a struggle between good and evil. Turkey and Greece also have a history of shadow puppetry, where plays are based on everyday life and contain much physical comedy. In Western Europe,

10 shadow puppetry enjoyed popularity during the 1800s when the art of cutting silhouettes out of paper was fashionable. In 1926, German shadow puppeteer Lotte Reiniger made the first full length animated film *The Adventures of Prince Achmet*.

15 Traditional shadow puppets are flat and made of leather. Areas within the puppet are punched out with sharp knives. These areas suggest

20 facial features and help define clothing. The puppets are made from separate pieces and joined together with wire or string. They are controlled by long rods and moved behind a white screen made from

25 paper or cloth. A lamp on the puppeteers' side of the stage provides the light: the audience on the other side sees the moving shadows. Cut-out areas within the figures allow light to shine through.

Contemporary shadow puppets may be made with a

30 variety of materials including paper, plastic, wood, coloured filters, cloth, feathers, dried plants or found objects ranging from silk scarves to kitchen utensils. Shadow puppets have also been made with three-dimensional wire heads and cloth bodies.

35 Contemporary shadow puppeteers might use many specialized lighting effects, including various theatrical lighting instruments, overhead projectors, reflected light, projected films, head lamps and hand-held lights.

OREGON SHADOW THEATRE, USA

Glossary

puppetry art of making and performing with puppets

epics long traditional or classic stories or poems, often made into plays

silhouette characters or objects cut out of black material

animated (in shadow puppetry) when cut-out figures or puppets appear to come to life by using strings or rods

Word origins

play (n), the meaning 'dramatic performance' originates from the early 1500s and the Middle Dutch word *pleien*, meaning 'rejoice, leap for joy'
Related words:
- playscript • playwright

drama (n), comes from a Greek word, *dráō*, meaning 'to do, to act'
Related words:
- dramatize • dramatic

- Recognize the structure and purpose of a text
- Communicate personal opinions confidently
- Write a playscript appropriate for the intended audience

Comprehension

A

1 The writer states that shadow puppetry is the 'oldest form of puppetry in the world'. Where was it first performed?
2 In what way did the 1926 film *The Adventures of Prince Achmet* represent a new form of film-making?
3 What are the 'long rods' in shadow puppetry for?

B

1 What is the purpose of this text?
2 Is the text a first, second or third person narrative?

C

1 Why is light important in shadow puppetry?
2 In what ways is modern shadow puppetry different from traditional shadow puppetry?
3 How do you think shadow puppetry might convey drama and emotion compared with other forms of theatre?

Talk about ...

Look at the shadow puppets and puppetry performances on these pages.

- What sort of stories do you think these shadow puppets would act out? What characters do you think they play?
- How do you think the traditions differ from country to country?
- What other art forms do they relate to?

Create your own shadow puppet play

Think of a story for young children. It could be an adaptation of one you know or a story that you have made up. Decide on the time and place in which it will be set.

- Cut the characters out of black paper to create silhouettes.
- Create three or more scenes for your play.
- Write a script to be read out.

Shadow play, China

Shadow play, Cambodia

7 Peace

Will there ever be peace on Earth?

> ❝ Peace cannot be kept by force. It can only be achieved by understanding. ❞
>
> ALBERT EINSTEIN

Talk about ...

- The word 'peace' can mean 'a situation or a period of time with no war, hostility or violence in a region' or 'the state of being calm or quiet'. Which meaning would you think of first?
- When did you last experience peace? Was it in a particular place, or with a particular person or animal?
- What does the quotation from Einstein mean?

Below are three more quotations about peace. Which definition of peace in the first 'Talk about ...' question is each referring to? Explain what they mean. Which quotation is your favourite? Why?

- 'When you make peace with yourself, you make peace with the world.'
- 'When the power of love overcomes the love of power, the world will know peace.'
- 'Peace begins with a smile.'

Word origins

peace (n), comes from the Latin word *pax*
Related words:
- pacify
- peaceful

Painting a peaceful scene

Close your eyes and listen to some peaceful music. Imagine a peaceful scene. What do you think of when you hear the word 'peace'? Perhaps peace for you is exemplified in a particular colour, or a quality of stillness, or something to do with nature. Or is it more to do with your state of mind?

Does the picture in your head look in any way like the scenes in either of these paintings?

- Join in a discussion and express personal opinions
- Explore the meaning of a word

Talk about ...
- Which of the paintings looks the most peaceful?
- What would you put in your picture if you were painting a peaceful scene?
- What does peace mean to you?

Over Eternal Peace, painted by the Russian artist Isaak Ilyich Levitan in 1894

Stretch zone

Discuss what you think the following phrases using 'peace' mean:
- 'keep the peace'
- 'be at peace with yourself'
- 'make peace with someone'
- 'hold your peace'.

Oil painting of an autumn forest

- Read and enjoy poetry set in a different time and culture
- Use implicit and explicit evidence from a text to answer questions
- Discuss how poets play with themes and conventions

Does peace mean no war?

When you were discussing what peace meant to you, did you talk about the absence of war? One way of encouraging peace is by discouraging or rejecting war.

Bulat Okudzhava (1924–1997) was a Russian folk singer and writer, who served as a soldier in the Second World War. In this poem, he gives advice to a young man who is keen to go off to war.

Don't Believe in War

Don't believe in war, lad,
you can never win a fight.
War constricts the heart, lad,
a pair of boots too tight.

5 Your mighty horses swift and true
will be no use at all
as, exposed upon a giant's palm,
beneath musket shot you'll fall.

Bulat Okudzhava

The Battle of Moscow 1941 by Evgeny Ivanovich Danilevsky

Comprehension

1 What three points of warning and advice is given to the lad in the first stanza?
2 What do you learn about war horses in the second stanza?
3 What is the inevitable fate that awaits the soldier?

1 In what way can war 'constrict the heart'? What image does the poet use to illustrate this?
2 Explain the effect of the metaphor in the second stanza.
3 What might a 'giant's palm' refer to?

Stretch zone

Look at the painting above by Danilevsky. Describe what you can see. What makes the conditions seem so harsh?

Glossary

lad boy or young man
constricts tightens or restricts the flow of something
swift fast
exposed made (something) visible by uncovering it
palm inside part of the hand
musket long-barrelled gun used in the sixteenth to seventeenth

The losses of war

Wilfred Owen (1893–1918) was an English poet who died in France in the First World War. In this poem, he writes about a dead soldier and the futility of war.

- Use implicit and explicit evidence from a text to answer questions
- Discuss how poets play with themes and conventions
- Present a poem using multimedia elements

Futility

Move him into the sun –
Gently its touch awoke him once,
At home, whispering of fields half-sown.
Always it woke him, even in France,
5 Until this morning and this snow.
If anything might rouse him now
The kind old sun will know.

Think how it wakes the seeds –
Woke once the clays of a cold star.
10 Are limbs, so dear-achieved, are sides
Full-nerved, still warm, too hard to stir?
Was it for this the clay grew tall?
– O what made fatuous sunbeams toil
To break earth's sleep at all?

WILFRED OWEN

Glossary

futility incapability of producing any useful result; pointless

sown plant seed by scattering it on or in earth

rouse wake (someone) up

clay here refers to what humans are made of

fatuous silly and pointless

toil work extremely hard

Comprehension

 A

1 Who does 'him' refer to?
2 Why does the poet want to move the body into the sun?
3 What do you think was the occupation of the dead soldier before the war?

 B

Look at the 'Language tip' on page 92 to help you.

1 What effect does Owen create by personifying the sun? What is the mood of the poem at this point?

2 How does the mood of the poem change in the last two lines? What do you think makes the poet feel like this?

 C

1 Do you think the two poems you have studied on this page and the previous page are powerful? Why? Why not? Do you think one worked better than the other? Do you know of any poets in your country who write about war?

Stretch zone

Choose one of the poems or a different poem about war. Draw or find a good picture to accompany it. Arrange the words of the poem around the picture to create a poster. Then write a paragraph explaining why you have presented the poem in the way you have. Be prepared to present your poster, using suitable background music if you wish.

- Read and enjoy a fable
- Develop a wide vocabulary through reading

Who fights like cats and dogs?

In fables, animals often personify human attributes. This is an extension of the use of simile and metaphor.

All animals fight amongst themselves. Fighting is a common instinct that we all share. But only humans take it to a higher level of organization that leads to wars.

The story you are about to read is an old fable from Myanmar which has been told many times, in many places and over many years. It suggests that the actions of human beings are ultimately responsible for war. What lesson can we learn from it?

The Drop of Honey

There was once a king who was eating his breakfast, sitting on one of the many palace balconies. His deep red silk robe was embroidered with gold elephants which sparkled as they caught the sun. He sat there, looking down onto his subjects
5   bustling about in the market in the street below. Breakfasting with the king was his trusted minister who came each morning to the king to tell him of the affairs of state.

The king particularly liked puffed rice for his breakfast. Over it he poured the delicious honey made by bees which collected
10   nectar from the lilies and orchids in the palace gardens. "Nothing can beat our honey," he said as he filled his mouth. "Only our bees can produce such delicate sweetness!"

"Indeed, that is so, Your Majesty," agreed the minister.

Just then, a drop of honey fell from the king's rice onto the
15   edge of the balcony. "Let me clean that up, Your Majesty," said the minister, bending forward with a cloth.

"Oh no," replied the king. "That's not our problem. Leave it to the servants." And so they continued with their breakfast, talking of this and that.

20   Meanwhile the drop of honey, warmed by the sun, dripped down below where people had set up their market stalls, fruit sellers wheeled their carts, and a shepherd stood with his herd of goats. Immediately a fly landed on the drop of honey and started its own breakfast. A green gecko noticed the fly. Its

Glossary

balconies platforms enclosed by a wall or balustrade on the outside of a building

embroidered decorated with patterns sewn on with thread

trusted regarded as reliable and/or truthful

market stalls stands or booths where goods are sold in a market

Language tip
Figurative language refers to a word or phrase not used literally but used to create a particular impression or mood. It includes the literary devices of **metaphor** and **simile**, but also **onomatopoeia**, **alliteration** and **personification**. Used well, figurative language will enhance your writing and is one of the ingredients that turns ordinary writing into literature.

- Read and enjoy a fable
- Work out the meaning of new words

25   tongue flicked in and out as it lurked in a dark crack of the palace wall. Suddenly the fly had disappeared down its throat.

     But a cat saw the gecko as it darted back into its dark hiding place. Cats are quick in their movements and before the gecko had reached safety, the cat had pounced on it. But a dog which
30   had been stretched out asleep in the shade was immediately awake. Up on his four legs in a second, he gave one ferocious bark and leaped on the cat which hissed and did her best to scratch the dog's eyes out.

     Up on the balcony, the minister was a little worried about the
35   commotion. "Your Majesty," he said, "there's a nasty cat and dog fight going on down there. Should we ask someone to go out and stop it?"

     "Don't worry," said the king. "Cats and dogs are always fighting. It's not our problem. Have some more of this wonderful honey."

40   Meanwhile, the owners of the cat and the dog had left their market stalls and were trying to separate their animals. But the cat's claws were vicious and the dog's teeth were dangerous, so the owners started to shout at each other. Then the dog's owner punched the cat's owner in the face. He, in turn, took
45   up a piece of wood and hit the dog owner over the head.

     The minister saw the situation with growing concern. "Your Majesty, I must insist," he said. "Those two men are fighting one another. Someone is going to be badly hurt. Shouldn't we call someone to break it up?"

50   The king looked down as he dabbed the honey from his chin with a crisp white napkin. "Leave them to it," he said languidly. "It's not our problem."

     Meanwhile, the fight below in the street had grown worse. Friends and family had gathered around the dog and cat owners.
55   To begin with, they cheered the two men on, but then the families started to join in. Soon the two groups were fighting each other. Stalls were upturned and some people lay groaning on the ground, holding their heads. Some men were wounded and bleeding.

Glossary

lurked hidden and waiting in ambush for someone or something

concern anxiousness or worry

Language tip

- Use figurative language occasionally. Too much lessens its impact. Make sure it is doing a job – enhancing the image you are trying to create.
- Choose literary devices carefully and make sure comparisons work. Obscure comparisons such as 'her cheeks were as soft as brown bananas' just sound wrong.
- If you are using figurative language as dialogue, be sure it is appropriate for that character. For example, a rough, tough character probably would not use elaborate language.

60 The minister was becoming increasingly distressed. "Your Majesty, we must do something! The fight in the street is getting worse!"

"Oh, do sit down, Minister!" replied the irritated king.

Now soldiers had arrived on the scene. At first they tried to
65 break up the fight, but then they also took sides. Some sided with the cat's owner and some with the dog's owner. The soldiers were armed and it wasn't long before one was killed. Soon the whole town was fighting, and the country had erupted into civil war. Houses were destroyed and the palace was set on
70 fire. Many people were killed and became homeless.

Days later, the king and his minister stood beside the charred ruins of the palace, and what was left of the town. "Perhaps I was wrong," said the king sadly. "Perhaps the drop of honey was our problem after all."

Glossary

sided with agreed with or supported the opinions or actions of someone

charred burnt and blackened

Comprehension

1 Describe the scene set in the first paragraph.

2 What happened during the king's breakfast that was to have such important consequences?

3 What did the minister want to do when he saw the cat and dog fighting?

4 What happened after the cat and dog started to fight?

5 What was the king thinking at the very end of the story?

1 Find two adjectives in the story that mean 'extremely fierce'.

2 Which word means 'lazily'?

3 Write down synonyms for 'erupted' and 'charred'. (lines 68 and 71)

4 Explain how the honey is used metaphorically in the story.

1 Discuss what the moral of 'The Drop of Honey' is and what it has to say about human nature. Use these questions to help you:

- Who is responsible for the war?
- Which animals behave most like humans?
- Why does the minister not want to contradict the king?
- Can you think of any sayings that might teach us something in response to this fable? For example, 'Do good to those in need' or 'Love your neighbour'.

Write a graphic novel

Draw a vertical line. This is your storyline. Mark in the fall of the drop of honey at the beginning of the line and the civil war at the end.

- With a partner, decide which are the ten most important events in the story between dropping the honey and the civil war. Mark these events along your storyline.

- Take it in turns to tell each other the story in your own words.

- Divide an A3 sheet of paper into 12 boxes. Draw one event of the story in each box and write a caption describing each event. Where appropriate, add speech bubbles to show what the characters are saying or thinking.

- Use implicit and explicit evidence from a text to answer questions
- Contribute to group discussion and listen to others
- Write a graphic novel

Language tip
When words like 'king', 'queen' and 'minister' are used as general terms, they are spelled out in lower case letters. However, when these nouns are names of actual people (proper nouns), they begin with a capital letter.

For example: 'The first king of Myanmar (then Burma) was King Anawrahta (1044–1077).'

Learning tip
A fable is a story that can be interpreted on two different levels. On one level, the story is about what happened after a drop of honey fell from the palace balcony. This is a literal reading of what happened. On another level, it can be interpreted as metaphorical, with a moral that aims to teach a more general truth.

Representing war in art

Read this art review about *The Mule Track*, a famous anti-war painting, which Paul Nash painted from sketches he made in 1918 on the Western Front during the First World War.

Paul Nash and war landscapes

The Mule Track, painted by Paul Nash in 1918

Glossary

incarnate fiend an evil being in human form

shells casing around explosives acting like a bomb

inarticulate unable to express one's ideas or feelings clearly or easily

"No pen or drawing can convey this country ... Evil and the incarnate fiend alone can be master of this war ... the black dying trees ooze and sweat and the shells never cease ... I am no longer an artist interested and curious, I am a messenger who will bring
5 back word from the men who are fighting ... Feeble, inarticulate, will be my message, but it will have a bitter truth ..."

This is what Paul Nash wrote in a letter to his wife Margaret from the Western Front, where he was working as an official war artist. After the outbreak of the First World War, Nash was sent to the Western Front in Belgium as an officer with the Hampshire Regiment. In the summer of 1917, he was injured and returned to London for treatment. During his recovery, Nash exhibited some of his drawings depicting the Western Front. As a result, he was commissioned to go back to Belgium as an official war artist.

While Nash had been away, the war at the Western Front raged on and, when Nash returned, he was horrified by what he saw. He was appalled by the destruction of the landscape and the suffering of the troops. In his notes, he wrote, "no one in England knows what the scene of the war is like … If I can, I will show them." When writing to his wife that his work was "feeble" and "inarticulate", Nash was not referring to his skill as an artist but his inability to portray the scale and intensity of carnage and suffering he was witnessing.

Nash's war work reflects a new approach to documenting war in art. No longer heroic, it seems more like a condemnation of the pointlessness and destruction of war. The drawings he made at the front are shocking, stark and bleak. Tiny figures move miserably across terrifying, desolate landscapes. Nash made dozens of sketches. Once back in England, he translated these into detailed drawings and oil paintings.

The Mule Track was one of those paintings. With its angular, harsh edges, the painting captures the horror of life at the front. Nash uses the influence of modern movements in art – specifically Surrealism and Cubism – to show how the natural landscape has been tortured by war into something grotesque and frightening. The scene is of a battlefield suffering heavy bombardment. The shattered landscape is severed by a jagged path, along which a mule train is trying to travel. The tiny figures, just visible in the distance, rear up in panic at a nearby explosion as water shoots up into the air. In the sky, there are huge clouds of yellow-grey smoke and rubble flying everywhere. In the centre of all the chaos, the poor, defenceless mules are at the mercy of forces outside their control in a hostile, alien landscape.

Glossary

Western Front one of the main areas of conflict in the First World War

appalled greatly dismayed or horrified

carnage killing of a large number of people

stark severe or bare in appearance or outline

severed having been cut or sliced off

Language tip

Irony is saying the opposite of what you mean in order to make a point, typically for humorous effect.

For example: 'Oh, what a lovely war!', when war is horrendous.

?

In 1918, the works of war artists had an enormous impact on the public. Do you think artwork remains significant in today's world? Why? Why not? Do we still use artwork to convey messages to the public? Explain your answer using examples if you can.

Stretch zone

We are making a New World is another of Nash's acclaimed war paintings. Find an image of it on the internet. Write a paragraph describing the painting and how the title is using irony.

Comprehension

1 Why was Paul Nash asked to become a war artist?

2 Why was he worried he would not be able to portray the war properly?

3 Why was Nash so shocked when he returned to the Western Front?

4 Explain how Nash's interpretation of war was different to war artists before him.

5 What is happening in *The Mule Track*?

1 Give an example of personification from the lines Nash wrote to his wife.

2 How does the writer use language to describe the impact the painting makes on the viewer?

3 Look at the way the writer has structured the review with paragraphs. What is the main topic of each paragraph?

1 Explain how adding the tiny figures of the mules intensifies the impact of the painting.

2 Nash used landscape to reflect the fear, anger and hopelessness the soldiers were feeling. Explain how he does this, using *The Mule Track* as an example. Think about the colour Nash uses and the way the natural environment such as trees are portrayed.

3 Nash's images helped to change perceptions about the war. Why do you think they had such a huge impact on the public in 1918? Do you think photographs would work just as well? Do you think *The Mule Track* remains a forceful image today?

- Use implicit and explicit evidence from a text to answer questions
- Explain metaphorical and symbolic meaning in a painting
- Explore using pictures to convey meaning

Stretch zone

Abstract art does not attempt to represent a realistic picture but instead uses shapes, colours, forms and marks to achieve its effect. Draw an abstract picture with the title: *The Horror of War*. Be prepared to explain your ideas.

Design a stamp for peace

The stamps shown use peace symbols to help celebrate world peace. Which of the symbols do you recognize? Design your own stamp to celebrate world peace. Look at the peace symbols on page 111 for more inspiration. Then describe your stamp and explain the design to a partner.

What is a peace symbol?

Here are some more symbols of peace. Find out more about where these symbols and images come from and how they came to represent peace. Work in a group, each researching particular symbols. Then present the results of your research in class in one of the following ways:

- Carry out research
- Write a report, using multi-media elements
- Make a presentation, using multimedia elements

1 Compile a report on the history of your chosen symbols using drawings, photos or reproductions of works of art. Present your report to the class. Make sure each member of the group has a turn to present some of the information.

2 Make a film or slide show of your peace images with a dialogue or music in the background. Present your film/slide show to the class.

A dove carrying an olive branch is a commonly used symbol for peace.

According to Scandinavian mythology, mistletoe is a symbol of peace and friendship.

This universally recognized symbol of peace originated as part of the Campaign for Nuclear Disarmament.

The peace lily's white flowers resemble white flags of peace.

The white poppy is used as a symbol of peace, and is often worn with the red poppy that symbolizes Remembrance Day (in memory of people who died in wars).

An origami crane.
The crane is a traditional symbol for peace in Japan.

1,000 cranes for peace

In the following article, you will learn how origami, cranes and peace came together in the life of one very courageous young girl in Japan.

The paper cranes of peace

There is a Japanese legend which says that whoever folds one thousand origami cranes will live a long life. This legend took on a new significance in 1955 with the death of a 12-year-old girl in Japan, Sadako Sasaki, who was born in 1943.

5 Towards the end of the Second World War in 1945, the USA decided to use an entirely new, untested weapon to force Japan to surrender. On 6 August 1945, a B29 bomber dropped the world's first atomic bomb on Hiroshima. The atomic bomb exploded 580 metres above the city centre at 8.15 am. Tens of

10 thousands of people were killed instantly by the blast. The death toll rose to between 180,000 and 200,000 over the following years as a result of the terrible after-effects of the atomic bomb.

One of these victims was Sadako Sasaki. She was a healthy,

15 athletic and lively child until one day, when she was practising for a big race, she was overcome by dizziness and collapsed. She was found to be suffering from leukaemia, a direct result of contamination by the atomic bomb when she was just two years old. Nowadays, some forms of childhood leukaemia are

20 curable, but in Japan in the 1950s, it was called the 'atom bomb disease', and known to be fatal.

More than anything else, Sadako wanted to recover and run races once again. Her best friend told her about the legend which said that anyone who folded one thousand paper cranes

25 would be granted a wish. Sadako's wish was to live a long life. She believed that every crane she folded represented a wish. So she used every scrap of paper which could be found for her to fold her cranes. Even as her friends alongside her in the hospital died, she kept on folding – but her wish changed. Now

30 she wished that this kind of atrocity would never happen again. There should be no more bombs or wars. Her wish was for peace, so that neither children nor adults should ever suffer and die like this again.

Red-crowned cranes in their wetland habitat

Glossary

cranes elegant, long-legged birds

atomic bomb bomb which uses the rapid release of nuclear energy to cause damage through heat, blast and radioactivity

death toll number of deaths

leukaemia form of blood cancer

35 Sadako managed to fold 644 cranes before she could fold no more. She died on 25 October 1955. Her classmates and family folded the remaining 356 cranes to bury with her. But her tremendous courage and hope had been an inspiration to all who came to know of her paper-folding. Her friends were determined that she should be remembered and that her wish
40 should be fulfilled.

Young people from all over Japan contributed money which for the project would ensure that Sadako
45 would never be forgotten. In 1958, a statue of Sadako holding a golden crane was unveiled in Hiroshima Peace Park. The wish of
50 the children who worked for the project is in the inscription at the bottom of the statue. It reads:

This is our cry
55 *This is our prayer*
Peace in the world

Today, the origami cranes have become a symbol of the wish for peace. People from all over Japan, and the world, fold paper cranes and send them to Sadako's monument in Hiroshima.
60 Across the road from Sadako's Peace Monument is the Flame of Peace. It will be extinguished only when there are no more nuclear weapons on Earth. Today it is still burning.

Glossary

inspiration cause of an (often creative) brilliant idea
unveiled removed a covering from a monument or work of art in a public ceremony
inscription words that explain who a memorial is dedicated to
extinguished (a fire or light) stopped burning or shining

Sadako's monument in Hiroshima Peace Park

- Use implicit and explicit evidence from a text to answer questions
- Contribute to group discussion and build on others' ideas

Comprehension

1 What is origami? What is its essential rule?
2 What did the Japanese legend say about folding origami cranes?
3 What were the immediate and long-term consequences of what happened in 1945?
4 How did Sadako's wish change as she folded her paper cranes in hospital?
5 How have Sadako's friends all over the world helped to keep her story and her wish alive?

1 Which word in paragraph 3 means 'ends in death'?
2 What word or phrase could you use instead of 'atrocity' in paragraph 4?
3 Explain the meanings of the following words: after-effects, contamination, dizziness, leukaemia. Write down a word or phrase which links all four words.
4 Why has the writer used a short sentence at the end of the text? What is the significance of this information?

1 Sadako's courage and hope inspired all who came to know her. Do you think that a statue of Sadako holding a crane in Hiroshima Peace Park is a good way to remember her? Is the statue a testimony only to the life of Sadako?
2 If you were asked to organize something to commemorate the life of Sadako and the message she wanted to share, what would you organize to inspire other young people?

Hold a dialogue on world peace

A dialogue is different to a debate. In a debate, we argue our case and challenge opposing views. In a dialogue, we seek to build a collective understanding of an issue by sharing our different perspectives.

In groups of three or four, hold a dialogue focused on the following question:

Is world peace achievable?

Make sure you listen carefully to the opinions of others and try to build on others' ideas in your responses.

Paper cranes laid at the foot of Sadako's monument in Hiroshima Peace Park

Word origins

origami (n), comes from the Japanese words, *ori*, meaning 'fold', and *gami*, meaning 'paper'. Origami is a traditional art form in Japan and has only one rule – no scissors and no glue.

Create your own image of peace

How do the cartoons on this page contribute to the debate on war and peace?

What would be your idea for a monument, symbol or cartoon that aims to promote peace? It could be something simple like Sadako's origami crane.

- Look for inspiration in your country's history and traditions. Is there an event or a person that particularly inspires you? You might choose a real person or a character of your own invention.
- Alternatively, you could choose an object from the past or the present, or something from the natural world.
- Draft a proposal for your monument, symbol or cartoon. Include a rough sketch of your design and a paragraph to explain the main features and what they mean.

- Carry out research
- Explore using pictures to convey meaning
- Write a proposal including a design

?

Do you think it is important for young people like Sadako to have a voice in the world?

"HOW COME THERE AREN'T ANY PEACE HEROES?"

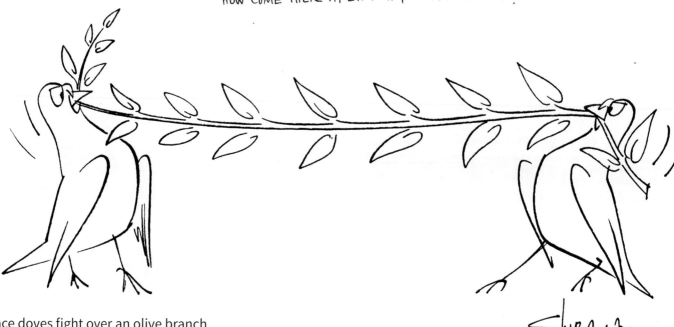

Peace doves fight over an olive branch

8 Looking back

What do we see when we look back?

> " I remember, I remember
> The house where I was born
> The little window where the sun
> Came peeping in at morn ... "
>
> THOMAS HOOD

Talk about ...

- What is the first thing that you can remember?
- Do you have vivid memories of the place where you were born?
- Can you remember a special occasion when you were really happy? What was so special about the event?

Make a list of all the places you can remember visiting before you were 12 years old (or around that age). Compare your list with your group.

Choose the place you remember most vividly and describe it to your group. Why do you remember it so well? Why were you there? What did you do while you were there? How does it feel to look back at the past?

Who are you? Where are you from?

Have you ever thought about what it means to be you? Have you ever been asked the questions in the title above? When people ask questions like these, they are trying to find out about you and your past. Knowing this will help them learn about what you are like. Everyone has good and bad memories and it's important to remember them because they are part of each person. People often like to tell stories and anecdotes about their past, which are sometimes funny or touching. Memories can be heart-warming, but also heart-breaking when remembering sad moments from the past.

- Talk about your memories
- Contribute to group discussion and listen to others

Stretch zone

Write a journal entry on one of your earliest memories. Why do you think you remember this scene from your life so vividly?

Language tip

In English, the heart is often used as a **metaphor** to express emotions.

For example: 'heart-broken', 'with a heavy heart', 'cold-hearted', 'half-hearted', 'heartless'.

Find similar words and add them all to your vocabulary list. Check their meanings.

Learning tip

Draw a large heart shape on a sheet of paper. As you work through this unit and read about different people's experiences, fill the heart with words which express their feelings.

- Read non-fiction
- Understand the structure and main features of a fact file

What's happening to my village?

Places and people change, often quite dramatically. 'The disappearing village' is one community's story, told from the point of view of one of its oldest inhabitants.

Seventy-year-old Peter John is a Yup'ik man living in Newtok, a village of about 320 people on the southwest coast of Alaska. The people of Newtok may become the first 'climate-change refugees'. The rise in temperature is destroying their village and they are going to have to leave and live somewhere else. Peter John looks back on his life as he talks to a reporter.

Glossary

permafrost layer of frozen soil many feet below the surface in polar regions that remains frozen all-year round

FACT FILE

Temperatures in Alaska have risen by 3°F (1.7°C) on average and 6°F (3.4°C) in winter. This is more than any other place on Earth in the last 50 years. The Arctic has experienced a rate of warming that is double Earth's average. This is because of 'positive feedback'. The brilliant white surface of snow and ice normally reflects most of the Sun's radiation back into space. But once the ice starts to melt, the exposed land absorbs the radiation, which causes further warming and melting. This affects the permafrost, which is thinning by more than one inch a year.

Map of Alaska

- Read non-fiction
- Work out the meaning of new words

Peter John at his home

The disappearing village

I've known for years that change was coming. The elders foretold it. As a boy I used to sit at the feet of my grandfather and my father, my great-uncles and my uncles as they sat in a circle in the *qasgiq* – that's the men's meeting house. Outside
5 the sea was one single thick block of ice and the snow lay thick on the ground. But inside I was warm as I listened to the discussion. Sometimes one of the elders would speak for an entire day! Nobody would interrupt him.

The elders, and the elders before them, had watched the land
10 and the sea for generations. They could see the change coming. They said the day would come when the Eskimos from our village and all along the coast of the Bering Sea wouldn't see winter again. "The snow will disappear," they said. Now these changes have taken place. When we were young the snow was
15 piled up so high that it reached the top of the schoolhouse. We used to use the snow as a ladder to climb up onto the roof! In those days the snow would lie thick until June. Now it's gone by April and geese from the south arrive months before they used to. In January and February, we used to take out dog teams
20 across the pack ice. We would dig through six foot of ice to fish below. Now there's only four foot. From this window I used to be able to see land stretching far into the distance. Now I can see the sheds where the salmon and herring are drying. I can also see those quad bikes which everyone runs around
25 on now! But more seriously, I see the water at the edge of the village where I used to see land. It's eating away at our village. Soon it will disappear.

Glossary

the elders group of senior men and women in a tribe or community who advise on and organize daily life

generation all the people born and living at about the same time, regarded collectively

quad bikes motorcycles with four large tyres, for off-road use

Language tip
When describing an **habitual action** in the past, you can say:

'We used to go fishing in the lake every summer.'

You may also use another construction:

'We would go fishing in the lake every summer.'

- Read non-fiction
- Work out the meaning of new words

30 Just look at the houses. Do you see how they are sinking? They're standing at all kinds of crazy angles. Do you see over there? That's where a piece of land collapsed into the sea not long ago. When I was young, the permafrost was our foundation as it had been for many thousands of years. But now it's melting and taking our village with it. Temperatures here in Alaska have risen more than any place on the planet in the last 35 50 years. The government is promising us a new village, but it isn't built yet. It will have a school and they say it will even have *naunnaviit* – that's patches of berries.

We have to have our *naunnaviit*! August was always the best month when I was young. It was berry-picking month. Blue, 40 black and red berries – there were so many from the bushes all over the hillside. We'd mix them with seal blubber and sugar and make wonderful ice-cream for our winter festivities. Winter was long back then and the festivities helped to make them seem shorter. The children still love picking berries. Our people 45 have a great respect for nature. We always have had. The elders in the past used to say, "If you come across a sick or dying animal, you must care for it. If you mistreat it, it will give you less and less." Seals, birds and fish – they all know what sort of person you are. If you make good use of them, they will 50 allow you to hunt them. But if you waste their meat or allow it to rot, then they will hide from you and you will be hungry.

Yup'ik children

- Use implicit and explicit evidence from a text to answer questions
- Use strategies to work out the meaning of new words
- Contribute to discussion and listen to others

Comprehension

A

1 Explain what effect the melting of the permafrost is having on the village.

2 Why have temperatures risen more in Alaska than anywhere else in the world?

3 What are *naunnaviit*? Why are they so important to the Yup'ik?

B

1 What does the verb 'foretold' mean? (line 2) What tense is it? What is its base form (infinitive)?

2 What does 'eating away at' mean? (line 26) What is eating away at what?

3 Discuss the meaning of the following terms and concepts in your group:
- pack ice
- permafrost
- climate-change refugees
- elders
- *qasgiq*
- positive feedback.

C

1 What kind of person do you think Peter John is? Give evidence from the text to support your answer.

2 The Yup'ik kill seals, birds and fish. You may think that it is cruel to kill animals. Why does Peter John think that is not so?

Language tip
The **plural form** of some nouns is the same as the singular form. They are usually names of fish or animals.

For example: 'salmon', 'herring', 'deer', 'moose'.

Stretch zone

Write a paragraph explaining why it is unfair that people like the Yup'ik are suffering the most from the effects of climate change.

Analyze a text

Read 'The disappearing village' again and make notes so that you can create a Venn diagram showing:

- Newtok when Peter John was young (in A)
- ways in which Newtok has not changed (in B)
- Newtok now (in C).

Add a heading for each section of the diagram.

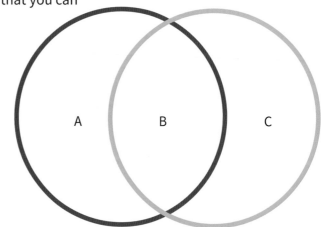

The Road Not Taken

Two roads diverged in a yellow wood,
And sorry I could not travel both
And be one traveller, long I stood
And looked down one as far as I could
5   To where it bent in the undergrowth;

Then took the other, as just as fair,
And having perhaps the better claim,
Because it was grassy and wanted wear;
Though as for that the passing there
10   Had worn them really about the same,

And both that morning equally lay
In leaves no step had trodden black.
Oh, I kept the first for another day!
Yet knowing how way leads on to way,
15   I doubted if I should ever come back.

I shall be telling this with a sigh
Somewhere ages and ages hence:
Two roads diverged in a wood, and I –
I took the one less travelled by,
20   And that has made all the difference.

ROBERT FROST

Learning tip
When reading poetry out loud, let the punctuation guide you. Pause for a short time for a comma, for longer and more deliberately with a semi-colon, and longest for a full stop. The only full stops in this poem come in the third stanza. The other lines run into each other without a full stop.

Language tip
We use **semi-colons** to separate clauses on the same theme within a sentence.

For example: 'It was raining very hard; the sea was lashing against the side of the cliff.'

Notice the semi-colon appears where the conjunction 'and' could have been.

- Understand metaphorical meaning
- Explain how language features create effects
- Contribute to discussion and listen to others
- Perform a poem, varying tone and volume, and using verbal and non-verbal techniques

Comprehension

1 What decision is the writer forced to make in the first stanza?
2 What makes the writer eventually choose the path he took?
3 Explain how the writer now has a different idea about both pathways.
4 How does the writer feel his choice of pathway affected his life?
5 What does the writer imagine himself doing in the future?

1 The images in the poem are metaphorical. What do you think the two different pathways represent?
2 The writer chooses the path which fewer people have taken. What might this represent metaphorically?
3 How do you think the writer feels now about the pathway he took? Give evidence from the poem to support your answer.
4 Which word best describes the tone of the poem?

1 Have you ever been forced to make a decision and then, after making it, wondered what it would have been like to have made a different decision? Are there decisions you regret making? Do you think about this a lot, or are you the type of person who says "what's done is done" and, if it can't be changed, you just need to get on with things as they are?

Language tip
Some words are often spelt wrongly. You could try a **mnemonic** to help you to memorize how to spell a tricky word.

For example: 'one collar and two sleeves'

This mnemonic could help you remember that the word 'necessary' has one 'c' and two 's's', which are the tricky parts of this spelling.

Perform a poem

You are going to perform the poem in pairs. Decide whether you want to perform it together or take turns to read separate stanzas. Think about the volume, tone and pace of your recital and the mood you want to create. Stand up to perform the poem and act out the scenarios as you describe them. Over-exaggerate your gestures and facial expressions.

The last time we visited

Things are about to change for Myung-ja. She lives with her family in Kangwon Province in Korea in the early twentieth century. Her grandparents are highly respected people who own a large estate. This extract tells of the wonderful day that Myung-ja and her brother Jin-ho share with their extended family, before they must move away to the city. Myung-ja must leave the place that features most in her memories of a happy childhood.

- Read and enjoy autobiography set in a different time and culture

Glossary

estate area of land and houses

Packard luxury US car that Anna's father liked to drive with the hood down

han-bok traditional, very elegant loose gown worn by Korean women

jugori and **paji** traditional long shirt and baggy trousers worn by Korean men

A luxury 1936 Packard car

A Korean woman wearing a traditional *han-bok*

- Read and enjoy autobiography set in a different time and culture
- Work out the meaning of new words

Visiting Grandfather and Grandmother

It was a beautiful, mild morning. Jin-ho and I were very excited about going to our grandparents' house. Not only was their seaside household filled with cousins, but the visit would involve a ride in the estate's glamorous black Packard, which my father
5 was borrowing for the day. Once we were out on the dirt road I pretended to be a princess, making a state visit. The landscape floated by as I waved to the cherry blossoms, pretending they were welcoming me. Sadly, we were only going six miles.

We drove slowly up a winding hill covered with tall pines and
10 there, on a cliff-top, lay my mother's family estate. Jin-ho and I cheered with excitement as Father drove around to the stables at the back of the house. We jumped out of the car and patted the horses. The air smelt deliciously sharp and salty from the sea. My mother gave Jin-ho a basket of honeyed rice cakes to
15 offer to our grandmother.

When we arrived, plump Grandfather Kang was out on one of the terraces in his elegant grey linen *jugori* and white *paji* trousers examining the leaf of an azalea bush. Like most Koreans, Grandfather had a deep love of trees. He had a
20 mulberry grove in which he cultivated silkworms. He also grew orchards of plum, apple, peach, cherry, pear, and nectarine trees. He had almond and walnut trees, persimmon trees, dates, bamboo and grapevines. In the autumn it was one of my favourite things to come with my mother and gather chestnuts
25 from beneath the chestnut trees.

Soon my grandmother, two aunts, and various cousins came out of the house to greet us with shouts and laughter. Grandmother, in a cream silk *han-bok*, was small, her hair in a tight black bun. My aunts were dressed more simply in pastel pink and
30 blue. After the luncheon feast, which my aunts had spent three days preparing, my two boy cousins, Jae-sung and Jae-dal, decided that Jin-ho and I would go down to the sea with them, a fifteen-minute walk away. Soon I could see and hear the ocean. My heart thumped in excitement. The air grew damper and
35 saltier against my face.

Language tip
Cohesive devices include conjunctions, connectives and pronouns which link ideas in a piece of writing. Using the same verb tense throughout a text also offers cohesion. For example, the conjunctions 'not only', 'but' and 'which' connect the ideas in this sentence:

'<u>Not only</u> was their seaside household filled with cousins, <u>but</u> the visit would involve a ride in the estate's glamorous black Packard, <u>which</u> my father was borrowing for the day.'

Pronouns also connect ideas without having to repeat the noun.

For example: 'The landscape floated by as I waved to the cherry blossoms, pretending <u>they</u> were welcoming me.'

An azalea in bloom

"Wait for me!" I cried.

But Jin-ho couldn't hear me. He was somersaulting down the hill, whooping and laughing and then hopping up and down barefoot on the shore next to his two cousins. The boys were
40 catching shrimps. I joined them at the inlet, trapping shrimps in my hands and putting them into the tin pail. When the water in the pail was thick with shrimps we climbed up the side of a hill, and Jae-dal made a small fire in a sand dune out of twigs and we roasted the shrimps. They were smoky, juicy and quite
45 delicious. Afterwards, we made our way slowly back up the hill to our grandparents' house.

The grown-ups were having tea and cakes on the veranda. Despite our little shrimp-feast, we crowded round the bamboo table like hungry baby birds as our aunts and grandmother
50 fussed over us. Grandmother sent us inside to wash our hands and faces. As I went to the kitchen I overheard Grandfather Kang talking to Father in his study.

"Yes, perhaps it would be wise to move to Seoul. It should be easier to find work in the city than here. Go and see. There
55 simply aren't the opportunities here."

Father was silent, then said, "Yes, I will have to sell up. I have no choice in the matter."

My mouth was dry with anxiety, heart pumping. It could not be possible. Sell
60 the farm? Leave our home? I ran into the empty nursery, and sobbed and howled. I felt as if life itself was being sucked painfully from my body. I cried until I fell asleep. I was still asleep when
65 we left for home in the evening. I refused to open my eyes. My heart was too heavy.

This, I remember, as my last day of childhood.

From *One Thousand Chestnut Trees* by MIRA STOUT

Word origins

somersault (n and v), meaning 'roll head over heels on the ground', comes from two Latin words, *supra*, meaning 'above', and *saltus*, meaning 'a leap'

Dasik, traditional Korean cookies flavoured with honey or pollen and often eaten with tea

Comprehension

A 👤

1 Why did Myung-ja say, 'Sadly, we were only going six miles'? (line 8)

2 Describe what the cousins did when they reached the sea.

3 What did Myung-ja overhear her father and grandfather saying? How did she react?

B 👤

1 How does the writer use sentence length to emphasize the moment when Myung-ja overheard her father and grandfather?

2 What does the word 'deliciously' tell you about what Myung-ja felt about the smell of the sea air? (line 13)

3 In lines 37–39, which verbs tell you what Jin-ho was doing? What do they tell you about his mood?

4 What picture in your head is painted by the simile 'like hungry baby birds'? (line 49)

5 Use a dictionary and the context in the text, to write a definition for each of the following words:

- glamorous (line 4)
- to whoop (line 38)
- state visit (line 6)
- tin pail (line 41)
- to cultivate (line 20)
- shrimps (line 42)
- silkworm (line 20)
- sand dune (line 43)
- pastel pink (line 29)
- to howl (line 62).

C 👥

1 What do you learn about Grandfather Kang?

2 How do you know that the grandmother and aunts thought that the visit was a special occasion?

- Use implicit and explicit evidence from a text to answer questions
- Use strategies to work out the meaning of new words
- Understand how texts reflect when and where they were written
- Role-play a story from a different point of view

Role-play the day's events

In groups of five, decide who will be each of the following: Myung-ja, Jin-ho, Father, Grandmother, Grandfather. Take it in turns to describe the day's events from your point of view. Ask each other questions and try to gain a greater understanding of each character's feelings and motivations.

- Write about a past event
- Write a composition using a range of sentence features
- Use various sentence lengths to create impact
- Use a range of cohesive devices to link ideas
- Proofread text and suggest improvements

Talk about ...

- A visit to your grandparents, or a friend or relative you feel close to. What is special about the place where they live?
- A time and place when you became aware that things were about to change. How did you know?
- Have you ever been to a special occasion where all your family and/or friends are really happy but for some reason you cannot help feeling sad? Can you explain why?

Write a composition

What incident or event in your past made a great impression on you? Perhaps it was a very big event, such as moving to another country or the birth of a baby brother or sister. Perhaps it was just a small incident, but it meant a great deal to you at the time. It may have been a happy event or a sad one.

Whether big or small, this event will be the inspiration for your composition. But what is more important is the way you write about it. All the words that you collected in your heart drawing will give you the vocabulary to help you express your ideas and feelings (look back to the 'Learning tip' on page 117).

Plan your writing in paragraphs. Make a paragraph plan with notes saying what each paragraph will be about.

Think about the following:

- writing about the incident in the past tense
- recording your thoughts and feelings about the events at the time
- using a mixture of short and long sentences for effect
- adding some figurative language, such as metaphor, simile or personification, for effect
- using some of the cohesive devices on page 125
- using a dictionary to make sure you spell words correctly.

In the final paragraph, write in the present tense to describe how you feel about the incident now.

Use your paragraph plan to write your narrative. When you have finished, proofread your own work before swapping your text with a partner. Proofread your partner's narrative for any grammatical, punctuation or spelling errors. Say what you like about the narrative and one thing that you would change to make it even better.

The Romantic poet William Wordsworth said, "the child is father of the man". Do you agree that our characters are moulded and formed from the experiences of our early childhood or do you think our characters go on evolving throughout life? Is there something you've experienced in the last few years that you think really influenced your character?

Looking back to books of the past

Before the printing press became common for printing books in Europe in the fifteenth and sixteenth centuries, oral (spoken) traditions of story-telling were common.

Books were very expensive as they were written out by hand. The people who wrote these manuscripts also decorated them very beautifully with illustrations and decorative borders and patterns. These are called illuminated manuscripts. *The Canterbury Tales* manuscript below is an example of an illuminated manuscript. *The Canterbury Tales* are a collection of stories written by Geoffrey Chaucer in Great Britain in the 1300s.

Illustrate a manuscript

Choose one paragraph from your composition. Write it out in your best handwriting.

- Add images and decorative features.
- Display your manuscript on a background board or frame, and present it to your class.

An illuminated manuscript of *The Canterbury Tales*

Word origins

manuscript (n), comes from two Latin words, *scriptum*, meaning 'written', and *manu*, meaning 'by hand' *Related words:*
- manual
- manufacture
- scripture

Talk about ...

- Look at the manuscript of *The Canterbury Tales*. What do you think the illustrations add to the reader's experience?
- What do you think the story being told is?
- Can you find any examples of more modern 'illuminated manuscripts', for example in some poetry collections?
- Why is it fitting that these illustrated manuscripts are said to be 'illuminated'?

How do people relate to different kinds of cats?

> 'Perhaps one reason we are fascinated by cats is because such a small animal can contain so much independence, dignity and freedom of spirit. Unlike the dog, the cat's personality is never bet on a human's. He demands acceptance on his own terms'
>
> LLOYD ALEXANDER

Talk about ...

- Do you think cats make good pets? Why? Why not?
- In what ways are domestic cats different from wild cats?
- Look at the insert image below. This famous image is a book cover. What kind of book do you think the cover is from? Explain why you think so. Do you think that it is an effective book cover? Why? Why not?

For centuries, black cats have played an important role in superstition, mythology and folklore. In many parts of Europe, black cats like the one on the right are considered unlucky even today. However, in Japan, black cats are a symbol of good luck. Now read about a classic black cat from France.

- Read non-fiction
- Understand how meaning can be conveyed in a picture
- Work out the meaning of new words

The story of a classic cat

Le Chat Noir

Its haughty gaze follows your eyes from wherever you look. No, I'm not describing the *Mona Lisa* but another iconic figure – the black cat from Swiss artist Théophile Steinlen's poster *Le Chat Noir*.

Today, the classic lithograph of *Le Chat Noir* is more famous than the venue it once proudly advertised. But that didn't used to be so. Le Chat Noir was a famous meeting place, founded by Rodolphe Salis in 1881 in the Montmartre area of Paris. The poster refers not only to the place but to the troop of entertainers who performed there. This troop specialized in unique pieces of shadow theatre inspired by Chinese shadow puppet shows. Bohemians and bourgeoisie alike flocked from near and far to the colourful, medieval-inspired interior to watch performances of the shadow theatre. Le Chat Noir attracted poets, actors, singers, musicians and other artists. For about 15 years, it contributed to making Montmartre the heart of artistic life in Paris.

The black cat stands proud and indignant, just like the rebellious, avant-garde clientele of Le Chat Noir. The image went on to become the icon of printmaking and of the culture of entertainment in Paris.

Glossary

lithograph type of print
bohemians unconventional people involved in the arts
bourgeoisie middle class, typically with reference to its materialistic or conventional attitudes
flocked congregated or gathered in large crowds
medieval referring to the Middle Ages (the fifth to fifteenth centuries)

Word origins

avant-garde (n), comes from the French language meaning the 'advance guard' and describes experimental or innovative art or design
clientele (n), a borrowed word from the French *clientèle*, whose modern meaning is 'customers'
Related word:
• client

Comprehension

1 Look at the two pictures of black cats on these pages. In what ways are they similar and in what ways are they different? Do you think one works better than the other as a design? Why? Why not?

- Read non-fiction
- Understand the features of an encyclopedia entry

The tiger

The tiger is the largest living cat species and a member of the genus *Panthera*. It is most easily recognized by its dark vertical stripes on orange-brown fur with a white underside. An apex predator, the tiger primarily preys on mammals such as deer and
5 wild boar.

Scientific name: *Panthera tigris*
Conservation status: Endangered (population decreasing)
Lifespan: 8–10 years (in the wild)
Speed: 49–65 km/h (adults, in short bursts)
10 **Mass:** 90–310 kg (adult males); 65–180 kg (adult females)

Tigers are highly adaptable and found in many habitats: open grasslands, tropical mangrove swamps and the Siberian taiga. They are territorial and generally solitary animals. They hunt across large areas of land to provide them with the meat they
15 need to live. However, they also live in some of the most densely populated places on Earth, and this has caused significant conflict with humans at times. All surviving species are under some kind of protection, but poaching and habitat destruction continue to be threats.

Glossary

apex predator animal that kills and eats other animals and is at the top of the food chain
carnivore predator and meat-eater

A Bengal tiger

- Read non-fiction
- Understand the features of a fact file
- Work out the meaning of new words

FACT FILE

- Tigers were once native to all continents except Australia and Antarctica. There are five remaining subspecies of tiger in the wild today.
- The Bengal tiger (*Panthera tigris tigris* or *Panthera tigris bengalensis*) is the most numerous and accounts for about half of the total tiger population. According to the World Wide Fund for Nature (WWF), there are about 2,000 Bengal tigers in the wild.
- The Siberian tiger (*Panthera tigris altaica*) is also known as the Amur, Manchurian, Altaic, Korean, North China or Ussuri tiger. Though it once roamed throughout Western and Central Asia and eastern Russia, it is now found only in the Amur-Ussuri region of Primorsky Krai and Khabarovsk Krai in far-eastern Siberia.
- The Siberian tiger is the largest and heaviest tiger, measuring up to 4 metres (13 feet) in total length and weighing up to 300 kg (660 pounds).
- The pelt (fur) of the Bengal, Indo-Chinese (*Panthera tigris corbetti*) and Sumatran (*Panthera tigris sumatrae*) tigers is a bright reddish tan, with dark, almost black, vertical stripes. The fur of the Siberian tiger is longer and paler. Unusual white tigers have been found, and even rare black tigers have been spotted in areas such as the forests of Myanmar and Bangladesh.
- Tigers hunt deer (sambar, chital and swamp deer) and wild boar. They have been known to attack larger animals such as elephants and water buffalo.
- Man-eating tigers are rare, but they are sometimes found in places like the Sundarbans and Nepal's Royal Chitwan National Park.
- Humans threaten tiger populations by killing tigers for their skins and other body parts, and by encroaching on their natural habitat.

Comprehension

A

1 What is the largest subspecies of tiger?
2 Explain why tigers are described as highly adaptable.
3 What are the main threats to tigers?

B

1 Use the context of the text to decide on the meaning of these words. Write a definition for each word.

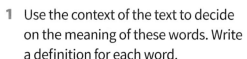

native	adaptable
territorial	populated
poaching	pelt

2 Look up each word above in a dictionary to see if your definition is correct.
3 What is the difference between 'coat', 'fur' and 'pelt'?
4 Identify any other unfamiliar words in the text. Look up their meanings.

C

1 Why do you think …
- the Siberian tiger has so many other names?
- it is a particularly difficult task to protect tigers?
- that people worldwide care so much about saving the tiger?

Looking at tigers in art

Look at the following examples of tigers in art. What qualities in the tiger do you think the artists wanted to emphasize?

Ghazi riding a tiger (above)

Bamboo and Tiger (above), painted by Nishimura Shigenaga

The Japanese artist Nishimura Shigenaga painted *Bamboo and Tiger* in the eighteenth century. It is a hand-coloured woodblock print. There were no tigers in Japan, so the artist was unlikely to have seen one in real life. In Japanese art, bamboo is a symbol of strength.

The scene showing a *ghazi* proudly riding a tiger was painted on paper and mounted on a cotton scroll. Scrolls such as these were used as visual props in storytelling performances in southern Asia around 1800 CE. There are 54 frames on this 13-metre long scroll, which shows the stories of Muslim saints *(pirs)*, including the Bengali Ghazi Pir who is shown above. Ghazi Pir, who fought dangerous animals, also had power over tigers.

Talk about ...
- What do you notice about the 'Japanese' tiger's posture and expression?
- Find out what a *ghazi* is. What is the impact of a *ghazi* riding a tiger?

- Understand how meaning can be conveyed in a picture
- Communicate personal opinions confidently

Surprised! (or *Tiger in a Tropical Storm*), painted by Henri Rousseau

Surprised! (or *Tiger in a Tropical Storm*) was painted by Henri Rousseau in 1891. It is the first of the jungle paintings for which he became famous. It shows a tiger, illuminated by a flash of lightning, preparing to pounce on its prey in the middle of a raging storm. The tiger's prey is beyond the edge of the canvas, so the viewer must imagine what will happen next.

The painting received mixed reviews. Some people did not realize the technical complexity of the work. Most critics initially mocked it for being childish. It seems simple, but the foliage has been carefully built up in layers, using a large number of green shades to capture the lushness of the jungle.

Stretch zone

Choose one of the paintings and write a description of it. Try to paint a picture with your words.

Talk about ...

What do you think the title of the painting refers to?

- The tiger's surprise at the lightning
- The tiger's prey's surprise at realizing the tiger is there
- The viewer's surprise at seeing the tiger (perhaps for the first time) lit up

Tiger, painted by Franz Marc

- Understand how meaning can be conveyed in a picture
- Communicate personal opinions confidently
- Write a review using appropriate style, tone and vocabulary

Talk about ...

- How is the strength of the tiger represented?
- What kind of mood do you sense from the position of the tiger?
- What do you think will happen next?
- Which of the representations of tigers on pages 134–136 do you like the best?

Tiger is one of the German artist Franz Marc's many works of animals in the Expressionist style. He painted it in 1912. The landscape is composed entirely of abstract, cubic forms painted in bright luminous tones. The tiger, recognizable from its dark stripes on yellowish fur, has been disturbed from its rest. It has lifted its head, its amber eyes fixed on … we don't know what. The viewer has to imagine what the tiger can see. Prey? Some sort of threat or danger?

Write a comparison review

You are going to write a review for an art magazine. You will compare and contrast two of the six works of art showing tigers and cats in this unit. Make notes on the following:

- Compare and contrast the styles of the paintings and/or prints. What is similar about them and what is different? How realistic is the representation of each tiger or cat, including its movement or posture? How well do you think the artist knew their subject?
- What do you think the artists are saying about human attitudes to tigers or cats? What do you think the artists' own attitudes to the animal is – sympathy, admiration, hostility, indifference?
- How similar or different are these images of tigers or cats to those you have seen on wildlife programmes on television or in a magazine article on wildlife conservation?

Use your notes to write your review comparing your two chosen artworks. Remember to use formal English and a style and tone that is suitable for readers of an art magazine. Present your review to the rest of the class.

- Read non-fiction
- Work out the meaning of new words

How can we protect people and tigers?

In the Sundarbans area of Bangladesh, villages are very close to the tigers' territory. Usually the tigers are afraid of human beings, but over the last couple of decades the tigers of the Sundarbans have started to hunt humans. Tigers are an endangered species and should not be killed, but the villagers need to protect themselves and their animals.

The web page on page 138 is about a project in the Sundarbans to help make it possible for human beings and tigers to live safely in close proximity to one another.

Word origins

mangrove (n), vigorous plant growing in forests and swamps in river estuaries in tropical parts of the world. Comes from the Spanish word *mangle*, the Portuguese *mangue*, and/or perhaps from a word in Carib or Arawakan, native languages of the West Indies.

?

Some experts say that it is impossible to save large animals such as tigers unless we protect the huge areas of land they roam in. Others say that the public care more for cuddly animals like pandas and striking animals like tigers than we do for reptiles and insects, although all are equally important. What do you think? Should we be directing our energies into saving bio-diverse areas or saving beautiful animals from extinction?

Dogs protect villagers from man-eating tigers in the
Sundarbans

World's largest mangrove

The Sundarbans form the world's largest mangrove forest. Extremely wild and inhospitable, it is an area where the tiger still reigns. It is also a <u>UNESCO World Heritage</u> site, so it should be a safe haven from humans. However, when food is scarce, local people enter the area to fish and hunt, and meet potentially dangerous tigers. Very sadly, the tigers now see humans as easy prey.

Tiger attacks on humans

Official figures show that at least 232 people were killed by tigers between 2001 and 2014. When a person is killed, family members and other villagers often hunt the tiger down. It's hardly surprising, therefore, that tiger numbers in the Sundarbans have dropped dramatically from about 440 tigers in 2004 to just 106 in 2015.

The difficult dilemma

The problem is that tigers need a large area in which to find sufficient prey to survive on. At the same time, their habitat is shrinking as human villages and activity take over. There are more than one million people living on the fringes of the Sundarbans and food is short for humans and tigers. The villagers allow their cattle to graze in the forest, which not only encourages tiger attacks but also lures tigers into the villages to find more cattle. As villages on the edge of the Sundarbans grow, resources diminish. The locals are poaching the deer and fish from the forests, and tigers are left to go hungry. Therefore, they attack humans.

Dog training

The <u>Zoological Society</u> in London is working with conservationists on various projects in the Sundarbans to try to save the tigers. One project trains stray dogs to act as an alarm when any prowling tigers come too close to the villages. By alerting the villagers to a tiger's presence, the tiger can be frightened away instead of being hunted and killed. Dog-training experts have been employed to train effective guard dogs from the shabby strays found scavenging in village bins. This initiative has been relatively successful as the strays are transformed from nasty nuisances to grand guardians of their communities.

Ending the bloodshed

There are so few tigers left in the wild that each one is precious. They are protected by law in Bangladesh, but it's hard to persuade people to value tigers when they are causing so much tragedy. But this problem must be solved. Otherwise the consequences will be disastrous for people and tigers. The tiger rules the forest. If the tiger goes, then the forest will go. If people can only find a way to minimize the threat, then perhaps the tiger can be seen for what it is – the region's greatest asset. Hopefully, tigers will find a lasting refuge in the Sundarbans.

5

10

15

20

25

30

35

40

45

50

55

60

- Use implicit and explicit evidence from a text to answer questions
- Write a web page, using appropriate style, structure and vocabulary

Comprehension

A

1 Explain what the conflict is between humans and tigers.
2 Describe one of the projects that conservationists have set up to try to solve the conflicts.
3 Explain how the stray dogs help to prevent tiger attacks.
4 Why is it so important to solve this problem both for people and tigers?

B

1 Look at the first paragraph. Which word tells the reader that people find the Sundarbans hostile? Which word refers to the saying that the tiger is king of the jungle?
2 In the fourth paragraph, which literary technique does the writer use to emphasize how the stray dogs change from pest to local hero? Give two examples from the text to support your answer.
3 In the last paragraph, the writer uses persuasive language. Explain how the language used is sympathetic to both tigers and the local people. How does the writer use persuasive language to make the final point?

C

1 Why do you think locals are being forced to hunt illegally in the protected area of the Sundarbans?

Be a web page designer

Create a web page for a wildlife conservation project in your region. Include details about:

- the current situation and the immediate action required
- what the local community feels about the problem
- what your organization hopes to achieve for the future.

Make your web page look authentic. Create an eye-catching heading or logo, and include pictures. Set out your material in an interesting way, for example by using headings, boxes and interactive links where readers can look up more information or contact the organization.

Talk about ...

- What do you think can be done to protect the villagers and the tigers in the Sundarbans?
- How can villagers and tigers help each other so they both have a future in or around the Sundarbans?

Language tip

The article often uses descriptive words to clarify information. It does this by using **noun phrases** that include adjectives to provide more specific detail. For example: 'man-eating tigers', 'stray dogs', and 'prowling tigers'.

Glossary

shrinking becoming or making smaller in size or amount

diminish make or become less

poaching take (animals, birds or fish) by illegal methods

scavenging searching for and collecting anything usable from waste or carcasses

initiative power or opportunity to act or take charge before others do

nuisances people or things causing inconvenience or annoyance

Communicating with animals

The story of Androcles and the lion was first told by Aesop, the writer of fables who lived in ancient Greece in 620–56 BCE. Since then, it has been retold many times in stories, plays and paintings.

- Read and enjoy fiction set in a different time and culture
- Develop a wide vocabulary through reading

Androcles and the Lion

It happened in ancient times that a slave named Androcles escaped from his master and fled into the forest. He wandered there for a long time until he was weary and almost dead from hunger and despair. As he lay resting beneath a tree, he heard a lion near
5   him moaning and groaning and at times roaring terribly. Even though he was so weak, Androcles got up and rushed away.

But as he hurried through the bushes, he stumbled over the root of a tree and fell down, twisting his ankle. When he tried to get up, he saw the lion coming towards him, limping on
10   three feet and holding its forepaw in front of it.

Looking more closely at it, Androcles saw a great big thorn pressed into the paw, which was the cause of all the lion's trouble. Plucking up courage, he seized hold of the thorn and drew it out of the lion's paw. The great beast roared with pain when the
15   thorn came out, but soon after found such relief that it rubbed up against Androcles and showed, in every way that it knew, that it was truly thankful for being relieved from such pain.

Instead of eating Androcles, the lion brought him a young deer that it had killed, and Androcles managed to make a meal from
20   it. For some time, the lion continued to bring what it had killed to share with Androcles, who became fond of the huge beast.

But their happy association did not last. One day a number of soldiers came marching through the forest and found Androcles, and they took him prisoner and took him back to the town
25   from which he had fled. There his master soon found Androcles and brought him before the authorities. Androcles was condemned to death because he had fled.

Now it used to be the custom to throw murderers and other criminals to the lions in a huge circus, so that the public could
30   enjoy the spectacle of a combat between them and the wild beasts. So Androcles was condemned to be thrown to the lions. On

Glossary

relief feeling of reassurance and relaxation following release from anxiety or distress

relieved reassured and relaxed following release from anxiety or distress

association group of people organized for a joint purpose

spectacle visually striking performance or display

combat fighting usually between armed forces

thereupon immediately or shortly after that

Androcles and the Lion, painted by Briton Rivière in 1908

the appointed day, he was led into the arena and left there alone with only a spear to protect himself from the lion.

35 The emperor was in the royal box that day and gave the signal for the lion to come out and attack Androcles. But when the great beast came out of its cage and got near Androcles, what do you think it did? Instead of jumping upon him, it rubbed up against him and stroked him with its paw and made no attempt to do him any harm. It was, of course, the lion which
40 Androcles had met in the forest.

The emperor, surprised at seeing such strange behaviour in so fierce a beast, summoned Androcles to him and asked him the reason for it. So Androcles told the emperor all that had happened to him and explained that the lion was showing its
45 gratitude for having been relieved of the thorn.

Thereupon the emperor pardoned Androcles and ordered his master to set him free, while the lion was taken back into the forest and let loose to enjoy freedom once more.

Comprehension

1 Why was Androcles hiding in the forest?
2 What was giving the lion so much pain?

1 'Thereupon' (line 46) is an old-fashioned word. What do you think it means? Can you find any other words in the text that are no longer used in modern English?

1 Why did the lion need to keep bringing Androcles food in the forest?
2 Who do you think shows the greatest compassion – the lion, Androcles or the emperor?

Talk about ...

- Aesop used to write the moral of the fable at the end of his stories.
  - What do you think would be the best moral to write at the end of this story?
  - What does it teach you about human behaviour?
  - Do you think there is more than one moral to this story?
- The lion, like the tiger, is often called 'king of the jungle'. Do you think the lion acts in a noble way?
- Why do you think the emperor chose to set both man and lion free?

What do Androcles and the lion say?

Draw a picture of Androcles and the lion in the arena with the audience and emperor watching. Add speech bubbles to show what the man and lion are saying to each other.

- Read and enjoy fiction set in a different time and culture
- Work out the meaning of new words

The writer and the lioness

This text is taken from a book called *Born Free* about a lioness named Elsa. *Born Free* is a memoir in which the writer, Joy Adamson, describes her real-life experience of living in Kenya, Africa, when she is asked to bring up Elsa as an orphaned cub.

Man and beast in trusting harmony

Close to the river stood a magnificent tree, its branches nearly sweeping the water. Under its green canopy, protected by its cool shade and subdued light from the
5   glaring sun, I felt as though I were under a dome. Here, concealed by the low branches, I watched many wild creatures, lesser kudu and bushbuck, which came to the river to drink, a hammer-headed
10   stork also came to quench his thirst and there were baboons; they provided the real fun. Sitting there with Elsa close to me, I felt as though I were on the doorstep of paradise; man and beast in trusting
15   harmony; the slow-flowing river adding to the idyll. I thought that this place would make a stimulating 'studio' for me to paint or write in, so we nailed some chop-boxes across a wooden frame and improvised
20   a table and bench, and soon I began to work there, leaning against the broad trunk of the tree.

Joy Adamson holding lion cubs

Glossary

canopy natural covering forming a shelter, for example of leaves and branches

subdued gentle and quiet

idyll beautiful or peaceful scene or situation

improvised make something quickly with whatever is available

- Read and enjoy fiction set in a different time and culture
- Work out the meaning of new words

Standing on her hind legs, Elsa inspected my paintbox and typewriter suspiciously; and resting both her paws on the
25 unfortunate tools, she licked my face and wanted to be assured of my affection before I was allowed to start work. Then she settled down at my feet and I began, full of inspiration; but I had
30 not reckoned with our audience. As soon as I tried to concentrate I heard the inquiring bark of a baboon peeping through the foliage; then the bush on the opposite bank became alive with
35 inquisitive watching faces. Soon, intrigued by Elsa, they came more and more into the open, swinging recklessly from tree to tree, screaming and barking, sliding backwards down the trunks or
40 hopping and swaying like shadows in the treetops, until one little chap fell with a splash into the river. At once,

- Read and enjoy fiction set in a different time and culture
- Work out the meaning of new words

an old baboon came to its rescue, and clutching the wet, struggling creature, raced off with it to safety. At this, all the
45 baboons in the world seemed to have got loose and the screeching was deafening. Elsa, who could tolerate the noise no longer, plunged into the river and swam across, accompanied by the hilarious shrieks of the baboons. As soon as she had reached firm ground she jumped at the nearest of the little tormentors.
50 He swung tantalizingly low but nimbly avoided a spanking by hopping to a higher branch, from which place of safety he pulled faces and shook the branch at Elsa. The others joined in the game, and the more infuriated Elsa became, the more they enjoyed teasing her – they sat just out of her reach –
55 pretending to be utterly unaware of the raging lioness just below. The scene was so funny that in spite of Elsa's humiliation I opened my ciné camera and filmed it. This was too much for her; as soon as she saw me focusing the hated box on her, she splashed back through the river and, before I had time to secure
60 the camera, she leapt on me and we both rolled over in the sand with the precious Bolex. Everything was wet; the baboons applauded our performance enthusiastically, and I fear that in the eyes of our audience both Elsa and I lost face very considerably.

After this the baboons looked every day for Elsa, and both
65 sides got to know each other very well. As she tolerated their provocations and took to ignoring them, they grew bolder and bolder. Often they squatted for their daily drinks
70 at the edge of the rapids, separated by only a few yards of water from her. One would keep sentry duty while the others sat on their haunches
75 and, bending low, slowly drank their fill.

From *Born Free* by Joy Adamson

Glossary

tantalizingly teasingly, tormenting something with something they want but cannot have

nimbly quickly, in an agile manner

ciné camera old-fashioned camera used to create moving pictures

provocations actions that make someone angry

Elsa

- Understand the development of ideas and themes in a text
- Identify how figurative language creates effects
- Understand how setting and characters are developed
- Write the last chapter of a story, using a range of sentence features

Comprehension

A

1 Explain what makes the spot chosen by the writer such a perfect place for her to work in? Give two ideas.
2 Explain why Elsa crosses the river.
3 Why did the baboons feel they got the better of both Elsa and the writer?

B

1 Why is a semi-colon used in line 11?
2 Why is the word 'studio' in quotation marks?
3 Give examples of the way the writer makes the baboons behave like people, *or* give examples of personification the writer uses to describe the baboons.
4 Why are dashes used in line 54?
5 What do the last lines of the text tell the reader about the relationship between the baboons and the lioness? Give two ideas and support each idea with evidence from the text.

C

1 Discuss the way the writer uses cohesive devices to connect ideas within paragraphs, across paragraphs and across the whole text.
2 What words would you use to describe the character and nature of the baboons?
3 What evidence is there in the text that the writer and the lioness are close?
4 Do you think wild animals can be tamed and live with humans or do you think they should always live in their natural habitat in the wild? Explain your answer.

Finish the story

Eventually, the writer decides that the best thing she can do for Elsa is to allow her to go back to living in the wild. Write the last chapter of the story where the writer and her friend spend three months reintroducing Elsa to the wilderness and helping her to learn what she has to do to survive there. End your chapter with Elsa happily disappearing off into the savannah. Use a wide range of cohesive devices so that your narrative flows smoothly and logically.

Language tip

With cohesion, sentences and paragraphs flow smoothly so the whole piece of writing is fluid and makes sense. Here are more cohesive devices:

Adverbials of place, time or manner help create cohesion in or across paragraphs.

For example: 'We went to sleep. The next day, we woke up to the sound of birds singing.'

Repetition can also be used as a cohesive device to highlight or emphasize important information.

For example: 'Leo was running late again. He had promised not to be late this morning. If only he could get to work on time for once!'

Repetition of 'late' helps create a sense of urgency across the sentences.

Synonyms allow the same idea to be repeated but in a different way, to create cohesion.

For example: 'Marta loved cycling in the countryside at the weekend. Cycling in the great outdoors gave her a sense of freedom.'

What keeps us going in difficult times?

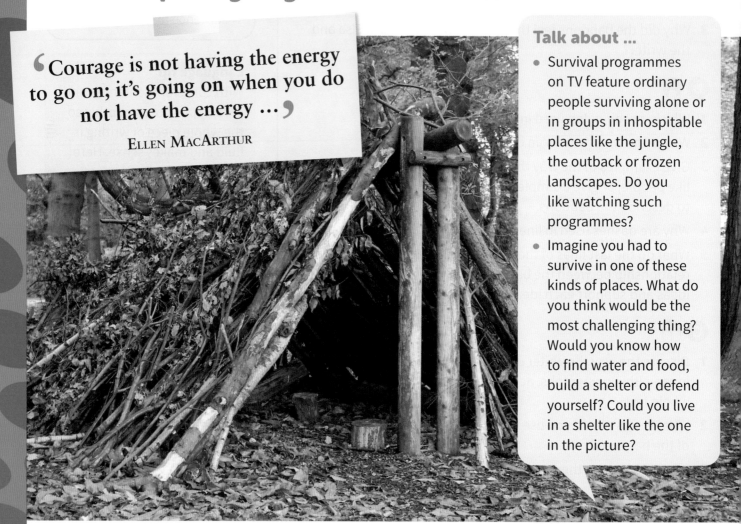

> 'Courage is not having the energy to go on; it's going on when you do not have the energy ...'
>
> ELLEN MACARTHUR

Talk about ...

- Survival programmes on TV feature ordinary people surviving alone or in groups in inhospitable places like the jungle, the outback or frozen landscapes. Do you like watching such programmes?

- Imagine you had to survive in one of these kinds of places. What do you think would be the most challenging thing? Would you know how to find water and food, build a shelter or defend yourself? Could you live in a shelter like the one in the picture?

Do you ever feel stressed? Most people experience stress sometimes, for example when taking exams, completing a project for a deadline, or performing a musical solo in front of an audience. That's just a normal part of life. However, too much stress can be bad for your health. Read the advice opposite about the different ways to reduce stress and to help you survive the ups and downs of life.

How is the text organized to make the information easy to read? The language is informal. How many different features of informal writing can you find?

With a partner, discuss which advice you think is the most useful and effective, and which ideas you think would not work. Decide on another good piece of advice to add to the list.

Word origins

stress (n), related to the Old French word *estresse*, meaning 'oppression, narrowness', which comes from the Latin word *strictus*, meaning 'drawn tight'
Related words:
- distress • constrict

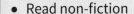

Seven ways to reduce your stress levels

Be in control of your external pressures

Are you doing too much? Are you doing too many after-school activities? Is there anything you can drop? Don't be pressurized to do things because other people want you to. Do what's best for you and your health.

5 ### Try to strengthen your emotional resilience

Don't let things get to you. So what if you didn't play your best game of football and your team lost. It happens sometimes – get over it and move on.

Use mindful methods to help

10 Take five minutes to pause and think. How are you feeling? Why are you feeling like that? Spend some time with a best friend or a sibling you get on well with – talk things through.

Get regular exercise

Experts agree – exercise is a great stress-buster and lowers anxiety
15 levels. You don't have to play in a team. Instead, go for a walk and admire the beauty around you.

Identify what is stressing you out

Work out exactly what it is that's causing you stress. Is it too much homework? Is it a school subject you're falling behind with? Are you
20 worried you're losing your best friend? If you work out what is causing stress, then you can begin to find ways to reduce it.

Organize your time carefully

If you organize your time efficiently, you might be surprised how much you can achieve. Try writing a list of all the things you need to do in
25 the day and number them from most important to least important. Then, if you get the most important work done, at least you'll feel more in control.

Accept that there are things you just can't change

Some things in life just can't be changed (your house might be in a
30 noisy neighbourhood, but there is nothing you can do to change this) – so try your best to ignore those things and concentrate on the things you can change.

Learning tip
Information texts are sometimes called non-chronological reports because they give information about something without mentioning the order in which things happen. The **features of information texts** include:

- main title
- subheadings
- paragraphs
- bullet points
- text in bold
- a layout that makes the information clear and eye-catching.

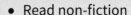

- Read non-fiction
- Work out the meaning of new words

One woman against the ocean

'If we could build an economy that would use things rather than use them up, we could build a future'

ELLEN MACARTHUR

Ellen MacArthur is a famous British yachtswoman. Following her retirement from professional sailing in 2010, Ellen announced the launch of the Ellen MacArthur Foundation. It's a charity that works with businesses and education institutions to promote a 'circular economy' – one that eliminates waste and pollution, and regenerates nature. Read the article below about Ellen and how she is now using her survival skills to try to help the planet survive.

Ellen MacArthur – Showing how we can thrive on limited resources

Ellen MacArthur became famous for triumphing in the face of huge adversity. On 7 February 2005, she broke the world record for the fastest solo circumnavigation of the globe.

5   The feat focused attention on the remarkable and sustained discipline you needed to achieve such a feat. Alone on a small boat in the immensity of the world's oceans, you were strikingly vulnerable. Bad conditions were guaranteed and you had to survive them. You had limited space to store all the things you were going to need to survive.

10 And you had to be alert, always. So essential was constant vigilance to success and survival, MacArthur could not allow herself to sleep for more than 20 minutes at a time. [...]

It was a feat of meticulous planning and preparation, for sure. It was a triumph of professionalism and care from the team that
15 surrounded her definitely. But ultimately – and this is what the wider public saw – it was a feat of personal strength and tenacity.

Her sailing career made MacArthur extraordinary, in an ordinary way. By that I mean she showed great sporting prowess, pushed herself to achieve what hadn't been achieved before, and by so
20 doing earned herself recognition and admiration from a wider

Glossary

circumnavigation sailing or travelling all the way around something, especially the world

feat achievement that requires great courage, skill or strength

immensity extremely large size, scale or extent of something

alert quick to notice any unusual and potentially dangerous or difficult circumstances

vigilance state of keeping careful watch for possible danger or difficulties

meticulous showing great attention to detail; very careful and precise

- Read non-fiction
- Work out the meaning of new words

public. That is the pattern we have come to expect of great sports people.

But she then did something that changed the picture completely. She reflected on the wider message behind her existence on such a limited base of resources while out at sea, and drew parallels with our wider situation living with a growing population on a finite planet.

She quit competitive sailing. She refocused her attention on the bigger challenge – seeking to popularize the idea that we need to create wealth, and find success as a species, within a much more highly constrained set of resources.

The Ellen MacArthur Foundation was created to promote the idea of a circular economy – a concept that existed in part through a handful of academics and think tanks – but which had not entered the mainstream in any meaningful way. [...]

Ellen MacArthur's approach has made the foundation one of the most effective advocates of its type. Her name recognition might have been enough to give it some cachet, but her commitment to the cause has been total. Her reflective influence has ensured that it has produced some of the more solidly based research and advocacy of any such groups, gaining the respect and attention of top business leaders and decision makers as a result. Her instinct for storytelling and narrative has meant that the foundation produces some of the best communications to make complex ideas seem simple. [...]

MacArthur stands out because, once the implications of what she had seen sank in, she devoted herself to finding a constructive alternative. Lighting a candle rather than cursing the darkness.

In that situation, it would be easy to take for granted the contribution that this powerful, smart and inspiring woman is making to our progress from the old world of make, use and waste, to a hopeful new one of make, use and renew.

She may be in the headlines less than she was when her achievement was her personal survival of the hostile seas. But what she is doing now is her most important work, and this time it's our survival that is the prize.

Glossary

finite limited in size or extent
constrained controlled or more focused in number
cachet having a special quality which people admire and approve of
constructive having or intended to have a useful or beneficial purpose
alternative available as another possibility or choice

Learning tip

To work out the **meaning of unfamiliar words**, first, look at the context – the rest of the sentence and especially the parts before and after the unfamiliar word. Try to identify the word class. Is the word a verb, a noun or an adjective, for example? Context should also give other hints, for example, if it's a negative or positive word.

Also think of similar words that are familiar. Examples: 'monster'/'monstrous'. Have suffixes or prefixes been added to a root word? Do you know their meaning? Can you work out what the root word is?

If you still can't work out the meaning, look the word up in a dictionary and keep your own personal vocabulary book.

Comprehension

A

1 What achievement made Ellen MacArthur famous?

2 In your own words, explain what the writer means by 'Her sailing career made MacArthur extraordinary, in an ordinary way.'

3 The Ellen MacArthur Foundation promotes the idea of a circular economy. Where did the ideas behind a circular economy come from?

B

1 Match each word or phrase from the text to the correct meaning.

Quotation from the text	Meaning
'in the face of huge adversity' (lines 1–2)	skill or expertise in something
'strikingly vulnerable' (lines 6–7)	state of serious or continued difficulty or misfortune
'tenacity' (line 16)	extremely fragile and exposed to danger
'prowess' (line 18)	quality or fact of being very determined; determination

2 'Lighting a candle' is metaphorical. Explain what the writer means by 'Lighting a candle rather than cursing the darkness.'

C

1 How do you think Ellen's experience as a yachtswoman has influenced what she is doing now? Think about …
- the kind of character needed to sail solo around the world
- what she learned about life while surviving on the open sea
- how she uses her experiences to get across the main messages of a circular economy.

- Use implicit and explicit evidence from the text to answer questions
- Work out the meaning of new words
- Contribute to discussions and communicate personal ideas confidently

 Stretch zone

Think of other good ideas to help businesses become more eco-friendly. Make a list. Choose your best idea and write a paragraph to persuade your target business why they should adopt your idea.

Should famous people raise awareness of important issues?

Discuss the topic below with a partner. Before you start, spend a few minutes making notes about your main points. When you think of an argument, try to anticipate what the counter-argument might be, and be ready to respond to it.

'It is the duty of famous people and celebrities to bring important issues to the public's attention.'

A story about leprosy

Leprosy is an infectious disease that causes parts of the body to waste away. It is very rare and treatable today. This book is set in 1906, on Culion Island in the Philippines where lepers were held to stop leprosy from spreading to others. Ami lived on the island with her mother. She doesn't have leprosy, but her mother does. At 12 years old, Ami is taken from her mother and sent to an orphanage on another island. This extract is the first letter that Ami receives from her mother.

The Island at the End of Everything: a letter

My dearest Ami,

My hand is bad so Sister Margaritte is typing this on her typewriter while I talk. I am sorry that this has taken so long. I have fallen behind on our letters already.

5   There are more and more people arriving every day. You can't imagine how busy the town is, and how confusing all the new *Sano* and *Leproso* rules are.

The hospital is very full and people aren't very happy. Now Mr Zamora has left, there is someone else in charge called
10 Mr Alonso. He is not much better, but at least he isn't so fearfully skinny.

I have made some new friends, though. My neighbour is a nice girl called Lerma. She reminds me of me, because she was taken from her family and is only twenty. She is from Mindoro Island,
15 which is where your *ama* was from.

Bondoc and Capuno are doing all right. I see Capuno most days and Bondoc came today. It took him two days to get permission and he wasn't allowed to touch us. I am not sure how we will

Glossary

Sano Spanish word for 'healthy', referring to the people without leprosy

Leproso Spanish word referring to the people with leprosy

ama father in Bikol (a language of the Philippines)

151

- Read and enjoy fiction set in a different time and culture
- Use implicit and explicit evidence from a text to answer questions
- Identify techniques used to hook the reader and create suspense

20 live like this but we will try. Hopefully when you come back they will have realized how silly they are being.

Apart from my hand and a small cold, I am in good health. They keep us busy with helping the arrivals, and soon the hospital is to be run only by Touched, apart from the nuns and Doctor Tomas. I am going to try to get a job there so I can send you some money.

25 I have some bad news, but you would want to know. Rosita passed away. I hope this doesn't make you too sad. Her suffering is over, and it was time for her. Her funeral was yesterday. It was in the church, unfortunately, but it was still a very lovely sendoff. I have apologized to Sister Margaritte for that remark
30 but won't let her cross it out.

Tell me everything. I hope it is beautiful and that you are well looked after. I will write again when Sister Margaritte can type for me. She is very busy at the moment so I can't write every day like I promised. Know that I want to.

35 I love you.

Nanay.

Glossary

passed away died
Nanay Mother in Bikol

Comprehension

1 Why is Sister Margaritte writing instead of Ami's mother?
2 Where does Nanay hope to find employment?
3 Why is Sister Margaritte so busy?

1 When the writer describes Nanay in the rest of the novel, it is always in the third person. Why do you think the author decided to include this letter in the first person?
2 What phrases does Nanay use to reassure Ami that everything is alright in her life?

1 Nanay is a leper, taken from her home, and her daughter has been taken away from her. Is Nanay just surviving? Or are there positive things in Nanay's life? Make a list. Is it possible to find positive things in any situation?

 Stretch zone

Imagine you are Ami. Write a letter back to your mother, describing your life in the orphanage and your new friend.

- Read and enjoy fiction set in a different time and culture
- Understand the development of ideas and themes in a text

The Island at the End of Everything (*continued*)

"Well?" says Mari eventually. "Is everything all right?"

My skin prickles hot, the letter's words burned behind my lids, like I've stared at the sun too long. This is not how I thought I'd feel after Nanay's first letter. I thought it would be something
5 warm and comforting, like a smooth river stone perfect to cup in a palm. This feeling is jagged and sharp. My whole body seems to shake with the strength of my heartbeat as I try to grasp the facts.

"Our friend, Rosita. She died."

10 "Oh, no, I'm so sorry."

"She was very sick. Nanay says it was better this way."

"And your *nanay*? Is she well?"

I stare down at the letter. "She has a cold."

"That's all right, isn't it? As long as she beats it before the
15 rainy season?"

I take a deep breath. "Yes, I suppose so. Only … only a complication like that – it's what Rosita had. When you're Touched, it's not the leprosy that kills you most of the time."

It's complications. Doctor Tomas explained this to us at school
20 the day he arrived from the mainland, the only volunteer to take up a post on the island of no return. I was six years old. "Being Touched makes your body less able to fight colds and sweats and other illnesses," he said. He did not have the worry lines then that he has now. We were still textbook cases to him,
25 not families. "You must take proper precautions. Complications like colds are what can make you very sick."

"I'm sure she will be better soon," says Mari.

"Yes." I steady my breathing. She is right. Nanay has made friends and Sister Margaritte is helping her write to me. She is
30 all right, though the changes sound like a nuisance. I wonder what Mr Alonso looks like. Because Nanay has said he is not skinny I picture him as fat. It is funny how my mind thinks in

It was thought in the early 1900s that contact with 'infected' objects might spread leprosy, so the inhabitants of Culion Island used a special currency.

153

- Read and enjoy fiction set in a different time and culture
- Use implicit and explicit evidence from the text to answer questions
- Identify figurative language

opposites. Like when she says Culion has gone from Mr Zamora to Mr Alonso, I think of Z to A. A backwards alphabet. And
35 I have gone from living in a place with sunrise, to a place of sunset.

Mari is so quiet next to me I can almost forget she's there. I like this about her, that she knows when not to talk. She is looking out over the sea, escaped wisps of her pale hair blowing
40 around her shoulders. She is the strangest and most beautiful thing I have ever seen.

Comprehension

A

1 How is Ami's reaction to her mother's letter different to how she thought it would be?

2 What is it in the letter that makes Ami concerned about her mother's health?

B

1 List the metaphors that Ami uses to explain her feelings.

C

1 What does it mean to be 'Touched'?

2 Why does Ami refer to the island as the 'island of no return'?

3 'He did not have the worry lines then that he has now.' Discuss what this observation tells us about Doctor Tomas.

Butterflies and a snake

The orphanage has been hiding the children's letters. Ami's friend, Mari, finds the letters and gives one to Ami. In this new letter, Ami discovers that Nanay is very ill and is staying in the hospital on Culion Island. Ami and her friends Mari and Kidlat escape from the orphanage and travel back to Culion Island to see Nanay. In this extract, the children are nearing the end of their long journey.

The Island at the End of Everything (*continued*)

- Read and enjoy fiction set in a different time and culture
- Identify techniques used to create suspense

We crawl, keeping our bodies close to the rocks, and lie on our bellies to peer over the top. Buildings come into sight – the backs of houses and the low-slung shadow of a fence. There were never houses this close to the forest before. I'm not sure
5 how we are going to get to the hospital without being noticed. I can hear Touched children laughing from the gardens ahead as the butterflies swoop around them. Culion is swarming with them. I hope Nanay has seen them.

I feel something light brush my face, and a large blue-and-white
10 butterfly lands neatly on the back of my hand. It opens and closes its wings once, twice.

"Ami." Mari says my name slowly. "Don't move."

"I know," I breathe. "It's amazing."

"No." Her voice is tight, a coiled spring. "Don't. Move."

15 Then I feel something else. A weight on my leg, moving across my calves. Slithering. My body tenses.

"Don't move!" Mari breathes.

I try to remember what Nanay told me about snakes. A hundred different kinds and only ten that are poisonous. The weight is
20 shifting up my thigh, and I try not to shudder as I feel it cross my lower back. My insides are locked in a silent scream. They won't do harm unless you do harm, like diwatas. Up the flat of my back now, and though it is impossible, I imagine I can feel the tongue flicking out across my back.

25 Mari has moved silently beside me to grab a large stone. I can see her hand from the corner of my eye, white-knuckled and shaking. Only ten poisonous. More scared of you than you are of it. The snake is
30 nearing my shoulders. I wonder if I can move fast enough to flick it off before it has a chance to strike. I should have kicked it off my leg. I focus on the butterfly, its wings opening a third time, a fourth, the eye at the centre of
35 each shimmering on each beat.

Language tip

Writers use a range of techniques to **build suspense**, including:

- giving hints to suggest what is going to happen or the danger to come – for example, 'Her voice is tight, a coiled spring.'
- not being able to see the action
- varying the length of words, sentences and paragraphs, including:
  - short words for sudden shocks
  - lots of verbs to convey action and a fast pace
  - very short paragraphs.

Glossary

slithering moving smoothly over a surface in a slightly zigzag line

diwatas mythological guardian of nature in the Philippines

The snake is over my shoulder, and it is all I can do to stop myself turning to look at it. I can see its head in my peripheral vision – a spade-like triangle. Through my panic comes a memory of a snake cornered in the kitchen, ready

40 to strike. A temple viper, said Nanay, opening the back door wide and leading me out of the house. Never anger it, best to leave it to find its own way out. The tongue flicks. Never anger it.

Definitely poisonous. A chill descends my spine, although I am
45 sweating in the heat. I can see Mari's hand clenching the stone tighter and suddenly the butterfly is lifting off my hand with a soft kiss of pressure and the snake strikes at it, fangs bared, piercing my skin.

A boiling brand burns down to my bones. And then Mari's stone
50 comes smashing on top of it and Kidlat is screaming and just before I fade into the pain I think how Nanay always kissed me better if I hurt myself, and how everything is the wrong way round.

From *The Island at the End of Everything* by KIRAN MILLWOOD HARGRAVE

A note on the text: Ami survives the snake bite and is taken to the hospital where Nanay is being treated. Nanay and Ami get to spend time together before Nanay dies.

Glossary

bared uncovered and exposed to view
peripheral vision all that is visible to the eye outside the central area of focus

Comprehension

 A

1 What does Ami remember about snakes?
2 What does Ami's friend Mari do to help her?

 B

1 The writer refers to different senses in this extract. List the senses she uses and an example for each.
2 Find examples of metaphors in the extract.
3 What is the effect of the metaphor in line 14?

 C

1 How are past and present interwoven in this extract? What effect does this have?

Be an illustrator

Divide a sheet of paper into four. Choose which you think are the four most significant scenes, one from each of the three extracts and the last from the scene in the hospital with Ami lying in a hospital bed next to her mother's bed. Illustrate each scene, adding a caption to each picture to describe what is happening.

Motivate a friend

In pairs, role-play one of the following scenarios between best friends. Then you could swap roles.

Student A Some important exams start next month but you haven't done any revision. You are sure that you are not going to do very well in the exams and think it's too late to start revision now. You can't be bothered to work for them.

Student B Reassure student A that they will do well in the exams if they work hard. Try to motivate them to start revision.

Student B You have been working extremely hard on a school assignment. After school today, you just want to go home and collapse. However, your friends want you to go to a sports practice to test out new tactics for a match tomorrow.

Student A Try to convince student B that they must come to the practice as you need to test out new tactics. Try to motivate them to find the energy to join in.

Stretch zone

Your friend is spending the summer holiday in the UK on an English course. They feel lonely and want to give up the course to come back home. Write a motivational letter encouraging your friend to stay and complete the course.

Learning tip

Do some research into amazing stories of survival or examples of animals who manage to accomplish incredible things to stay alive. Use these examples to inspire your friend to keep going!

Newly hatched olive ridley sea turtles start life with a fight for survival, pulling themselves along the sand to reach the safety of the sea.

- Read and enjoy poetry
- Work out the meaning of new words

If at first, you don't succeed — try, try again!

The truth of the saying above has been recognized throughout the ages. Read these two poems on the same theme, both written by nineteenth-century American poets.

Don't Give Up

If you've tried and have not won,
Never stop for trying;
All that's good and great is done
Just by patient trying.

5 Though young birds, in flying, fall,
Still their wings grow stronger,
And the next time they can keep
Up a little longer.

Though the sturdy oak has known
10 Many a wind that bowed her,
She has risen again and grown
Loftier and prouder.

If by easy work you beat,
Who the more will prize you?
15 Gaining victory from defeat,
That's the test that tries you.

PHOEBE CARY

from Keep Tryin'

[...]

There are times when all of us
Get riled up and start a muss,
But there ain't no use to cuss,
Just
5 Keep Tryin'.

When things seem to go awry,
And the sun deserts your sky,
Don't sit down somewhere and cry,
But
10 Keep Tryin'.

Everybody honours grit,
Men who never whine a bit –
Men who tell the world, "I'm IT"
And
15 Keep Tryin'.

Get a hustle on you NOW,
Make a great, big solemn vow
That you'll win out anyhow,
And
20 Keep Tryin'.

All the world's a battlefield
Where the true man is revealed,
But the ones who never yield
Keep Tryin'.

EDWIN C. RANCK

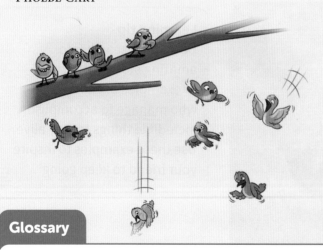

Glossary

riled up upset or angered by someone else

cuss speak angrily

grit courage and strength of mind to continue

whine long, high-pitched complaining cry

yield give way to arguments, demands or pressure

- Use implicit and explicit evidence from the text to answer questions
- Explain how language features create effects
- Compare poems on the same theme

Comprehension

A 👤

1 In stanza 1 of 'Don't Give Up', what quality does the writer say you need to do great things?
2 In the last stanza, what does the writer say is the most important life lesson?
3 Look at 'Keep Tryin'. What do people with true grit do?
4 In the last stanza, what does the writer say is the most important thing in life?

B 👤

1 Try to use the context of the poems to work out the meaning of the following:
- loftier (line 12, 'Don't Give Up')
- muss (line 2, 'Keep Tryin'')
- to go awry (line 6, 'Keep Tryin'').

The next three questions refer to 'Keep Tryin'.
2 Explain what the metaphor 'the sun deserts your sky' means in the poem.
3 What does the writer mean by 'I'm IT'?
4 Why does the writer compare the world to a battlefield?

C 👥

1 The phrases 'don't give up' and 'keep trying' are very similar in meaning. Is the tone of the poems similar? What other similarities can you find? In what ways do you think the poems are different?
2 Which poem do you like the most? Why?
3 What kind of things do you say to your friends if you want to motivate them when they are feeling down or worried?

?

The message in 'Keep Tryin' is that if you have real strength, you never give up until you win. The message in 'Don't Give Up' is that sometimes you have to admit defeat but learn from your mistakes. Which message do you agree with most? Are there times when both messages are correct? Who helps you keep going when times are hard? How important is it to have other people's support?

Who survives?

This unit is all about survival. But are those who survive 'survivors' or 'survivers'? Read this poster about how to remember some of the tricky spellings in English.

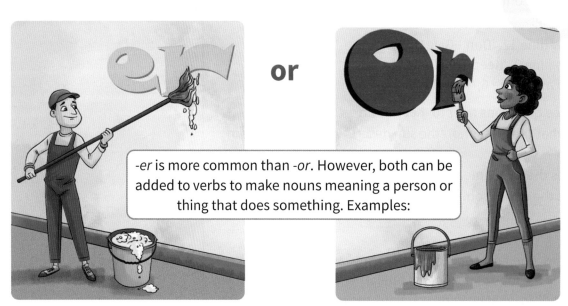

HOW TO SURVIVE
TRICKY SPELLINGS!

or

-er is more common than -or. However, both can be added to verbs to make nouns meaning a person or thing that does something. Examples:

clean/cleaner, build/builder, sprinkle/sprinkler, keep/keeper

survive/survivor, decorate/decorator, escalate/escalator, invigilate/invigilator

The -er ending can also be used to form nouns with the following meanings:

• a person or thing that has a particular quality or form. Examples: backpacker, three-wheeler, top scorer
• a person belonging to a particular place or group. Examples: native speaker, prisoner
• a person concerned with a particular thing. Examples: jeweller, lawyer, treasurer, fire fighter

There are no real rules about when these nouns have an -or or an -er ending. So just try to learn the most common words of each category.

- Develop strategies to spell difficult words correctly

Simple ways
to remember
TRICKY SPELLINGS

NECESSARY

Mnemonic

You can use mnemonics to help you memorize specific things, like how to spell a word. Example: to remember the tricky parts of 'necessary', think of a shirt – one collar and two sleeves. This will remind you that 'necessary' has one 'c' and two 's's.

Acrostic

You can also use an acrostic, which is a phrase you create from the letters that make up a difficult word. Example: to remind you how to spell 'because' you could remember 'Big Elephants Can Always Understand Smaller Elephants'.

separate

Words within words

Remembering shorter words within the tricky word can help. Example: 'separate' has 'a rat' within it.

Sound it out

It can be helpful to sound out the tricky parts of a word. Examples: 'Wed - NES -day', 'Feb-RU-ary'. Even if the word isn't pronounced like this, emphasizing certain sounds can help you remember the correct spelling.

What spelling rules do you know?

Can you think of any common rules for spelling, such as 'i before e except after c'? What about the rules for any of the following:

- adding suffixes to words that end in 'y'
- the silent 'e'
- double consonants
- plural suffixes
- words ending in -*ful*
- adding -*ly*?

Choose one of the rules that you are familiar with and explain it to a partner.

11 Secrets of the sea

What lies beneath the ocean waves?

> ❝ The Ocean has its silent caves,
> Deep, quiet, and alone;
> Though there be fury on the waves,
> Beneath them there is none ❞
>
> From 'The Ocean' by NATHANIEL HAWTHORNE

In the second half of the nineteenth century, the English poet Tennyson wrote a poem called 'The Kraken'. He imagined the kraken as a gigantic creature living at the bottom of the sea for thousands of years, which would one day come to the surface. See if you can work out the meaning of unfamiliar words from the context.

The Kraken

Below the thunders of the upper deep,
Far, far beneath in the abysmal sea,
His ancient, dreamless, uninvaded sleep
The Kraken sleepeth: faintest sunlights flee
5 About his shadowy sides; above him swell
Huge sponges of millennial growth and height;
And far away into the sickly light,
From many a wondrous grot and secret cell
Unnumbered and enormous polypi
10 Winnow with giant arms the slumbering green.
There hath he lain for ages, and will lie
Battening upon huge sea worms in his sleep,
Until the latter fire shall heat the deep;
Then once by man and angels to be seen,
15 In roaring he shall rise and on the surface die.

ALFRED LORD TENNYSON

Talk about ...

- Have you heard of the kraken? What other mythical sea creatures do you know about? Why do you think there are so many stories of these creatures all around the world?

- What makes the sea such a good setting for speculation about undiscovered creatures?

Glossary

abysmal bottomless
sleepeth old-fashioned word for 'sleeps'

What is a kraken?

Stories of a giant sea creature like a gigantic octopus or squid have been told for centuries. This enormous legendary sea monster was said to appear off the coasts
5 of Norway, Angola and other places. It was called a kraken. In German, *krake* means 'octopus' and, in Swedish, it means 'deformed animal'.

A creature of sailors' superstitions and
10 myths, the kraken was first described by the Norwegian bishop Pontoppidan in 1752. The bishop described the kraken as an octopus (polypus) of humungous size and wrote that it had a reputation
15 for pulling down ships.

It was, however, nineteenth-century French naturalist and artist Pierre Denys de Montfort who brought the kraken fully into the public's imagination with his
20 drawings of a huge octopus-like creature attacking a ship.

The great man-killing octopus then entered French fiction in 1866 when novelist Victor Hugo introduced the *pieuvre* octopus of
25 Guernsey lore. He compared it with the legend of the kraken, and this led to Jules Verne's depiction of the kraken, which was something between a massive squid and octopus.

30 The legend may well have originated from sightings of giant squid, which can grow to 13–15 metres in length.

Le Poulpe Colossal ('The Colossal Octopus'), showing a ship in the embrace of a monstrous squid, painted by Pierre Denys de Montfort in 1801

Talk about …

Why do you think people are so interested in creatures from the deep sea? Do you think there are still weird and wonderful creatures that we have yet to discover? How large do you think some of these deep-sea creatures might grow?

- Read non-fiction
- Recognize the structure of an article

Read all about it!

The following article is a report from an online magazine about an amazing catch by fishermen in New Zealand.

Glossary

calamari rings slices of squid for frying

Monsters from the deep

They're huge. They're ferocious. They were – until now – reassuringly rare. But the capture of a spectacular colossal squid could be a symptom of something bigger.
5 **Kathy Marks reports.**

A New Zealand fisherman with the colossal squid caught in the Southern Ocean. It is thought to be the largest ever found.

It is one of the most mysterious creatures of the deep ocean, and one of the most elusive. Only half a dozen colossal squid have been caught. The specimen hauled out of the waters of Antarctica weighed 450
10 kilograms, with eyes as big as dinner plates.

The gigantic sea creature, at least 15 metres long, with razor-sharp hooks on the end of its tentacles, was feasting on a Patagonian toothfish when it was caught by New Zealand fishermen. Experts described
15 it as a 'phenomenal' find. One said that if calamari rings were made from it, they would be the size of tractor tyres.

Colossal squid are in fact not related to giant squid, which grow to a maximum of 'only' 13 metres. They are not only larger than giant squid, but also meaner. 20 They are active and aggressive killers, and have been known to attack sperm whales.

While the giant squid has suckers lined with small teeth on the end of its tentacles, the colossal squid has two rows of rotating sharp hooks on its eight 25 tentacles. Its tentacles surround a parrot-shaped beak which is strong enough to cut steel cable. The beak and the hooks are a lethal combination.

The New Zealand Fisheries Minister who announced the discovery of the new specimen said it took 30 fishermen two hours to land it. They had been fishing with long lines for Patagonian toothfish in the Southern Ocean. The Minister said, "The squid was eating a hooked toothfish when it was hauled from the deep." The crew stopped long lining and manoeuvred the 35 squid into a cargo net to haul it in. It was then frozen on board and brought back to New Zealand for analysis. Experts have yet to examine it, but they believe it to be the first intact adult male ever landed.

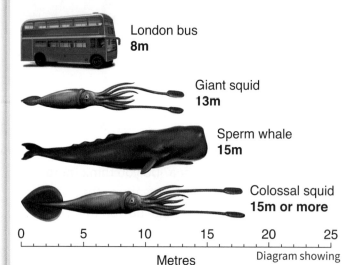

London bus
8m

Giant squid
13m

Sperm whale
15m

Colossal squid
15m or more

0   5   10   15   20   25

Metres   Diagram showing comparative lengths

Comprehension

1 Give one example of a fact and one example of an opinion from the second paragraph. (lines 6–10)

2 Colossal squids have been caught before. What is special about this one landed by New Zealand fishermen?

3 How did the fishermen manage to land the squid?

4 What 'lethal combination' does the colossal squid have?

1 Look at the opening words 'They're huge. They're ferocious. They were – until now – reassuringly rare' in the first paragraph. What technique has the writer used? Explain what effect it has.

2 What is 'reassuring' about the rarity of colossal squids?

3 Look at the third paragraph (lines 11–17). Give an example of a passive verb form. Why is the passive used here?

4 Look at the second and fifth paragraphs. Which details tell you how strong the colossal squid's beak is and how big its eyes are?

5 Discuss the meaning of the following words: ferocious, reassuringly, colossal, symptom, elusive, to feast on, phenomenal, aggressive, to rotate, lethal, intact. Then discuss your answers with a partner. Check the meanings of any words you're not sure about in a dictionary.

1 What would a conservationist's response to this article be? Should we let strange creatures get on with their own lives? Or is there a valid reason to catch rarely seen animals so we can study them and learn more about our world?

Measure the length of a squid

How big is a colossal squid? First, look at just how big a giant squid is. Stand with both your arms outstretched. Ask another student to measure from one fingertip on one hand to the other. If the measurement is about one metre, get 13 students to stand with arms outstretched fingertip to fingertip and see just how long a giant squid is. What about a colossal squid?

- Use implicit and explicit evidence from a text to answer questions
- Work out the meaning of new words
- Contribute to discussion and communicate personal ideas confidently

Word origins

manoeuvre (v), meaning 'move or manipulate something with great skill', comes from a Latin word, *mani*, meaning 'hand', and a French word, *œuvre*, meaning 'work'
Related words:
- manipulate
- manufacture

Language tip

You can use the 'not only … but also' structure in your sentences to compare two things or to further emphasize their difference.

For example: 'Colossal squid are not only larger than giant squid, but also meaner.'

The depths of the ocean are known as Earth's last frontier. Why do you think that is? Do you like the idea that there are still unexplored areas of our planet or would you like to know exactly what lurks in the ocean depths? Would you rather explore outer space or the depths of the ocean? Why?

Different ways of presenting information

Read this comic strip to learn more about one of the most colourful and fragile animals of the sea. Can you name all the other sea creatures illustrated in the comic strip? Then read the fact file on octopuses. What are the advantages and disadvantages of both ways of presenting information?

CORAL IS THE CONCRETE-LIKE SKELETON OF TINY MARINE ANIMALS, AND THESE SUBMARINE JEWELS ARE THE MOST DIVERSE ECOSYSTEMS ON EARTH

OVER MILLIONS OF YEARS THESE POLYPS HAVE BUILT STRUCTURES THAT SURPASS IN SCALE THE ARCHITECTURE OF ANY LIVING CREATURES—INCLUDING HUMANS

ONE OF THE MANY BENEFITS OF CORAL REEFS IS THAT THEY LIMIT THE DAMAGE FROM HURRICANES AND TSUNAMIS... AND BESIDES BEING THE HOME FOR MILLIONS OF FISH, THEY CONTAIN BIOMEDICAL AND OTHER RESOURCES THAT WE'VE ONLY BEGUN TO EXPLORE

THEY ARE THE BASIS FOR A MULTIMILLION DOLLAR TOURIST AND FISHING BUSINESS, BUT THEY ARE IN **TROUBLE**

BLEACHING FROM WARMING WATERS FOLLOWED BY DISEASE IS KILLING ANCIENT AND DELICATE CORAL FASTER THAN SCIENTISTS HAVE EVER SEEN

NOAA SEA SURFACE TEMPERATURE FIGURES SHOW THE SUSTAINED HEATING IN THE CARIBBEAN LAST SUMMER AND FALL WAS BY FAR THE WORST IN 20 YEARS OF SATELLITE MONITORING

JACK ELROD

THE BIG PROBLEM FOR THESE BEAUTIFUL STRUCTURES IS THE QUESTION OF WHETHER THEY CAN ADAPT SUFFICIENTLY AND QUICKLY ENOUGH TO COPE WITH CLIMATE CHANGE— LET'S HOPE THEY CAN

FACT FILE

Octopuses ...

are very old. The oldest known octopus fossil is 296 million years old. So octopuses were already well established long before life on land had progressed beyond insignificant pre-dinosaur reptiles.

have three hearts. Two of the hearts work to move blood beyond the animal's gills, while the third keeps circulation flowing for the organs.

have arms with a mind of their own. Two-thirds of an octopus's neurons are in its arms; the rest are in its head. This means the arms can solve how to open a shellfish while the octopus is busy doing something else, like checking out a cave for more edible goodies.

squirt ink. The ink hides the octopus but can also harm its enemies. It contains a compound called tyrosinase, which causes a blinding irritation when sprayed into a predator's eyes.

have blue blood. So they can survive in the deep ocean, octopuses evolved a copper-based blood called a haemocyanin. It turns their blood blue.

- Use explicit evidence from a text to answer questions
- Research a topic and make notes
- Create a comic strip, using a model

Comprehension

1 What is coral?
2 What benefits does coral offer to humanity?
3 What problems and dangers are coral facing?
4 Why is an octopus's blood blue?

1 Why do we need to look after the ocean? Whose responsibility is it?

Create your own comic strip

You are going to create your own comic strip to describe some of the ocean creatures that live in or around the sea. Your target audience is 10–11-year-old schoolchildren.

First decide whether you will describe one or more creatures. Then decide whether you want to write about sea birds, mammals or fish. You may choose to use the octopus fact file on page 166 as a starting point.

- Find out all you can about your chosen creature(s). Make lots of notes and collect pictures.
- Decide which information you are going to put into captions, how you will illustrate the information and how many boxes you will need in your cartoon strip.
- Make sure you vary the size of your cartoon boxes.
- Write a rough draft of the captions first, then add them to the relevant place in your cartoon strip using your best handwriting.
- When you have finished drawing your pictures and writing your captions, present your cartoons in small groups.
- Make a classroom display of the cartoons.

Talk about …

- How would you present the fact file facts about octopuses as a cartoon strip? What illustrations would you include?
- What can we do to make our seas and oceans healthier? Do you think there should be a total ban on commercial fishing for a few years while the seas recover? Should trawling methods be banned? Do you have any other ideas?

- Read and enjoy autobiography set in a different time and culture
- Work out the meaning of new words

What if you could not see the sea?

If you live in a land-locked country, the experience of seeing the sea for the first time must be amazing. But imagine what it must be like 'seeing' the sea for the first time if you are blind.

The extract you are about to read is about a young boy, Vedi, born in a region of what is now Pakistan. He contracted meningitis at the age of four and was left totally blind. His father wanted his son to have the best chance in life and he sent him 1,300 miles away to a boarding school specifically for blind and partially sighted children. There he was to learn English and braille.

The principal, Mr Mohun, wanted his pupils to have the same educational opportunities as sighted children, including sport and outings. In the following text, Vedi goes on a school trip to experience the sea for the first time in his life.

Our trip to the sea

One warm day, there was a series of explosions at the front gate. At first, I thought someone was setting off firecrackers, but then I realized that what I heard was a motorcar engine backfiring. We heard such engine sounds all the time mixed
5 with the clip-clop of horses, the clatter of handcarts, and the clink and ponk-ponk of bicycle bells and car horns. They were the sounds of passing traffic. No vehicle, it seemed, ever stopped in front of the school.

Glossary

totally blind with no vision at all

firecrackers loud, explosive fireworks

backfiring vehicle or engine undergoing a mistimed explosion in the cylinder or exhaust

Vedi listens to the sounds of the city street outside

10 "Mr Mohun wants us all at the front gate!" Bhaskar cried, running into the boys' dormitory. "There's a lorry! We are really going to the beach!"

We had heard Mr Mohun mention the visit to the beach and we had all talked about going to the seaside, without knowing exactly what it was.

15 "Why are we going in a lorry?" I asked.

"Because there are no trams to the beach, you son of an owl," Abdul said. "It's really far."

The lorry had no seats, so we all sat on the floor, the boys on one side and the girls on the other. I wanted to run around but 20 Mr Mohun was addressing us from the front of the lorry.

"Boys and girls, this is our first annual holiday at the beach," he said. "We have a day's holiday. I want you to stay in your places, because the ride is bumpy."

To help us pass the time, Miss Mary led us in a new song. It 25 really only had one line: 'John Brown's Bottle Number One Hundred and One'. Each time we sang it, we would sing out one number less than the time before. The song sounded festive to us, and we felt we were really on an annual holiday.

At the beach, I heard a sound I'd never heard before – a gigantic 30 roar alternating with the sound of a huge amount of water rushing out. I wanted to run towards the sound and touch it, and to feel what it was really like, but the Sighted Master herded us boys into the boys' shack. He gave us each a pair of bathing trunks and we got into them.

35 "Now you can do what you like," the Sighted Master said. "But don't go beyond the rope in the water."

I hesitated for a moment, wondering how, amid the roar and the rush, I would hear the Sighted Master ringing the bell on the other side of the rope. But the partially sighted boys started 40 running toward the roar and the rush, calling back, "Abdul, Reuben! Vedi! There is nothing in the way! You can run, too!"

I ran towards the roar and the rush. The air smelled of salt and coconut. There was hot, grainy, dry ground underfoot. It was

Glossary

annual yearly

alternating more than one thing occurring in turn repeatedly

Sighted Master teacher who can see

shack roughly built hut or cabin

hesitated paused in indecision before saying or doing something

partially sighted with some sight

- Read and enjoy autobiography set in a different time and culture
- Work out the meaning of new words

45 so hot that I could scarcely bear to put my feet on it, so I had to run fast, and couldn't stop to examine it. Suddenly, I was in the water, being carried out. It closed over my head. I forgot everything. I felt I'd never been so happy. A jolt opened my mouth. I was rapidly swallowing water that tasted of tears – buckets of them. I was flung back, choking. Again the water

50 closed over my head. The water retreated. I lay on the water, wondering how far the water could take me. Then I came up against the rope, as thick as the one we used for the tug-of-war, and I heard the Sighted Master calling to me, "That's far enough! Come back! You'll drown!"

55 We spent the day bathing in the water and running around on the new ground. I couldn't get over the way it shifted around, almost like the water. We could go into the water as often as we liked, and when we ran we just had to keep the sound of the ocean to our left or right, depending on which way we

60 were facing. The school compound suddenly shrank in my mind, like a woollen sock Mother had knitted for me which became so small after it was washed that I could hardly get my hand in it.

From *Vedi*

Glossary

flung thrown or hurled forcefully

retreated moved back or withdrew

tug-of-war game played by two teams competing to pull each end of a rope until the rope is pulled a certain distance or one team gives up

school compound institution or building where children under 19 receive education

Comprehension

1 In the first paragraph, Vedi heard the sound of backfiring. Why was this sound different from all the traffic sounds he usually heard?

2 What did the sea sound like to Vedi?

3 How did Vedi respond to the new experience of sand and sea?

4 Why did Vedi say the water 'tasted of tears'? (line 48)

5 How did the Sighted Master prevent the children from going too far out in the sea?

6 How did Vedi's thoughts about the school change when he was in the water?

1 Which words and punctuation in the second paragraph tell you that the children were excited?

2 Which literary technique is used in the sentence 'I ran towards the roar and the rush' and what effect does it have? (line 42)

3 How did Vedi describe the feel of the sand? Why did he call it 'ground' and not 'sand'? (line 43)

4 How does a sock shrunk in the wash describe Vedi's experience?

1 Read through 'Our trip to the sea' again. Make a list of the words and phrases that tell you that Vedi is using his senses of smell, touch and hearing instead of sight. With a partner, compare lists.

2 Do you think the trip to the sea will have changed Vedi's impression of the world? Why or why not?

Describe what cannot be seen

Think of an object. It could be as small as a grape or as big as an aeroplane. Describe it to a partner, who has their eyes closed. Use your senses of smell, touch and hearing. What does it feel like? What does it smell like? What does it sound like? Can your partner guess the object?

Once you have both described your objects and guessed what they are, discuss how it felt relying on all your senses apart from sight. Was it liberating, or was it frustrating? Talk about what you will take away from the experience.

- Use implicit and explicit evidence from the text to answer questions
- Understand the development of ideas and themes in a text
- Understand how characters are portrayed by their actions and dialogue

Language tip

Several sentences in 'Our trip to the sea' contain clauses that use the word '**so**' to introduce the result of an action or situation.

For example: 'The lorry had no seats, so we all sat on the floor …'

The word 'so' can also be used as an intensifier, as in 'so hot'.

 Stretch zone

Write a paragraph about a school trip you went on or one you wish you had gone on. It may have been a pleasurable experience – or not!

- Read and enjoy poetry set in a different time and culture

How happy are fish?

In China, fish symbolize wealth and happiness. They are, therefore, a popular subject in Chinese art and craft work. Do some research and see how many images of fish you can find in Chinese paintings and on porcelain.

This poem is a dialogue poem. It is a conversation between two fishermen who have different views about the happiness of fish. It has been translated from Chinese.

The Joy of Fishes

Chuang Tzu and Hui Tzu
Were crossing Hao river
By the dam.

Chuang said:
5   "See how free
The fishes leap and dart:
That is their happiness";

Hui replied,
"Since you are not a fish
10 How do you know
What makes fishes happy?"

Chuang said:
"Since you are not I
How can you possibly know
15 That I do not know
What makes fishes happy?"

Hui argued:
"If I, not being you,
Cannot know what you know
20 It follows that you
Not being a fish
Cannot know what they know."

Chuang said:
"Wait a minute!
25 Let us get back
To the original question.

What you asked me was
'How do you know
What makes fishes happy?'
30 From the terms of your
    question
You evidently know I know
What makes fishes happy.

I know the joy of fishes
35 In the river
Through my own joy, as I go
    walking
Along the same river."

CHUANG TZU,
translated by THOMAS MERTON

Chinese porcelain-covered jar with fish and seaweed design

Freehand painting of fish and flowers by Chinese artist Qi Baishi (1864–1957)

Comprehension

A 🧑

1 Describe the scene in the poem.

2 What does Chuang say at the beginning that prompts Hui to question the logic of his statement?

3 How does Chuang reply to Hui?

4 Do you think these are logical arguments? Why? Why not?

B 🧑

1 Explain how Chuang twists the meaning of Hui's original question to make it help his own argument. Focus specifically on the language used.

2 How would you describe the mood of the poem? Support your answer with evidence from the poem.

C 👥

1 In the poem, the two fishermen use persuasive arguments to express their points of view. Which do you think is the most persuasive? Why?

2 Who do you agree most with, Chuang or Hui? Why?

Be a poet

Write your own dialogue poem using two persuasive arguments for and against something.

- Think of a scenario in which two people present opposing points of view on a topic.
- Write a dialogue poem, using 'The Joy of Fishes' as a model.
- Use persuasive language to present both sides of the discussion. Make it a good experience by presenting well-rounded arguments on both sides and end on a positive note.

Chinese fisherman

- Use implicit and explicit evidence from a text to answer questions
- Discuss the features of dialogue poetry
- Write a poem, using a model

Language tip

There are two common uses of the word '**since**'. It can indicate time, as in 'since the time that …'

For example: 'I have not seen my sister since she emigrated to Australia.'

'Since' can also be used to mean 'because' or 'seeing that'.

For example: 'Since you are not a fish, how do you know what makes fish happy?'

Language tip

Persuasive texts are written to make the reader either agree with the writer's opinion, or do something. To be persuasive, the writer will often talk directly to the reader and may use the following literary devices:

- repeated words
- rule of three
- alliterative words
- emotional language
- rhetorical questions
- similes or metaphors
- humour.

Hunting a white whale

The novel *Moby-Dick* was written by the US writer Herman Melville and was first published in 1851. It is a story about a big white whale. In this extract, you will meet Ahab, the captain of a whaling ship called the *Pequod*. The crew are Fedallah, Starbuck, Tashtego, Stubb, Bildad and Queequeg, the harpoonist, a native from the South Seas, and Ishmael (who is the narrator of the story). In this extract, Pip, a galley-boy who was born into slavery, finds himself in a terrifying situation.

- Read and enjoy fiction set in a different time and culture
- Develop a wide vocabulary through reading

Glossary

quest long or difficult search for something

clatter make a continuous rattling sound like hard objects striking each other

plume long cloud of smoke or vapour resembling a feather

spouted stream of liquid issued with great force

gleam soft light, indicating hope or humour

bore down moved directly towards someone or something in a purposeful or intimidating manner

scribbling writing or drawing carelessly or hurriedly

The quest for Moby Dick

"There she blows! The White Whale!"

I thought at first, that I had dozed off to sleep and dreamed it. Then we heard Ahab's ivory leg clatter across the deck above, and he was bawling for us to turn to. I shook Queequeg's
5   hammock to wake him – but he was already on deck, while the rest of us collided on the ladder, and emerged on deck shivering in our shirts and bare legs.

Fedallah hung way out from the rigging, over the oil-black sea, his finger pointing. There, on the moonlit horizon, a geyser of
10   silver spray rose, fanned out, and drifted in veiling spray. The palest of outlines became visible beneath the surface of the sea, where the plume had spouted and there was no doubting it – a white whale, and within half a mile.

Ahab was on his quarterdeck
15   shouting commands. There was a gleam in his eyes. "Raise the sails! Up! Up! Steer for the spout. Lay on more canvas, I said! Put your backs into it! Put on more sail!"

20   Again the whale spouted – a sight so beautiful that grown men gasped. Three times it showed us its white cockade of water. The sight certainly taunted Ahab. "Make after him,
25   why don't you!" We bore down on the spot as fast as sail and wind would carry us.

A nineteenth-century woodcut of a Right whale spouting

- Read and enjoy fiction set in a different time and culture
- Work out the meaning of new words

30 Then it was gone. By the time we crossed the spot where the white whale had spouted, the water was no more remarkable a colour than any other stretch of night sea.

Later, Queequeg sat sharpening the barb of his harpoon, the tattoos on his face scribbling out all expression. "Tonight," he said. "He will come tonight." So he did. And the night after too. At the very same hour on the second watch, Fedallah cried
35 out from his mast-top perch and again the snowy fountain of glistening spray blew in shreds across the moonlit sea.

"He beckons me onwards," murmured Ahab on his quarterdeck, but we all heard him. "Moby Dick beckons me onwards to the Last Battle. Well, lead on, brute! I'll grasp you yet."

40 His hands reached out involuntarily in the direction of the whale-spout, and closed on the empty air. He was like King Arthur reaching for silver Excalibur. If he could once close his fist round that plume of spray, he would inherit such powers, such dominion. Like it or not, I was part of Ahab's quest. So
45 was every man aboard. We were his company of knights within the tiny kingdom of the Pequod and he could send us out to fight whatever dragons or monsters threatened his dominion.

One day, one of the oarsmen sprained his hand and could not row. "Pip shall go in his place," decreed Bildad who, as a part-
50 owner, did not want a penny's profit lost because of a boat short-handed.

Glossary

perch object on which a bird or person sits
involuntarily without consent or conscious control
sprained wrenched or twisted the ligaments of a joint, causing pain and swelling

Comprehension

A

1 What was the writer's first sighting of the whale?
2 What does Queequeg predict will happen?

B

1 How are the writer's and Ahab's reactions to the whale spouting completely different?
2 Give a quotation that shows that Ahab believes this is a personal vendetta between him and the whale.
3 Why does the writer liken himself to one of Ahab's knights?

Word origins

dominion (n), meaning 'territory of a sovereign or government', comes from the Latin word, *dominium*, meaning 'property belonging to the lord, master'
Related words:
• dominate • domineer

The quest for Moby Dick (*continued*)

So Pip was put into the boats. He was small for his age, and as he was lowered down the ship's side, he looked no more than a little boy, rigid with fright. He was born into slavery, and put up no kind of protest or plea for pity. The knuckles
5 of his black hands showed white as he ripped the oar. The blade flailed. He missed the water and fell off his bench. He dug too deep and dropped his oar. But Stubb, rather than heaping insults and abuse on him, in his usual way, only told him to be a "good, brave boy," and to do his best.

10 The first outing, Pip did nothing wrong, and the smile crept back to his lips. But the second time we gave chase to a whale, things did not go so smoothly. We were after a Right whale – so called because it swims slowly and floats when it's dead, which makes it the 'right whale to hunt'. Tashtego threw his
15 harpoon, and it struck, good and sound, behind the eye. The whale – as whales will – gave a twitch, and thrashed its tail against the bottom of the boat; it happened to hit the boards directly under Pip's seat. Thinking the boat would be smashed to pieces, he leapt up in terror – clean over the side, taking
20 with him the length of the harpoon rope as it began to pay out. The whale bolted, the line went taut. It coiled tight round Pip's chest and neck, and his lips turned instantly blue as he was towed along, sometimes above water sometimes below, caught in a knot somewhere between the running whale and
25 the boat it was towing.

"Wretched boy!" yelled Tashtego, drawing his knife. He glanced at Stubb, who hesitated for a moment. He liked Pip. But there again, the whale was big. The profits from it would be good. Boys are two-a-penny.

Glossary

flailed beaten with a short heavy stick swinging from a wooden staff

Whalers off Twofold Bay, New South Wales, painted by Oswald Walters Brierly in 1867

- Use implicit and explicit evidence from a text to answer questions
- Understand how characters are portrayed by their actions and dialogue
- Write a narrative from a different point of view

30 "Cut!" ordered Starbuck, from the middle of the boat, and Tashtego cut through the harpoon rope. The whale escaped. Pip was saved. But we cursed him for losing us the whale! Starbuck pulled the boy out of the water by his shirtfront and bellowed in his face. "Do that again, boy, and I shall leave thee
35 to drown, I promise thee! We've had precious few whales this voyage, without having to give one up for the likes of thee! We'll cut no more ropes for thee, dost comprehend me?"

I liked Starbuck the better for giving the order to cut. We were all fond of Pip. Yes, I liked Starbuck the better for pitying him.

From *Moby-Dick; or, The Whale* by HERMAN MELVILLE (retold by GERALDINE MCCAUGHREAN)

Word origins

comprehend (v), comes from the prefix *com-*, meaning 'together', and the Latin word, *prehendere*, meaning 'grasp or seize with the mind'
Related words:
- comprehensive
- apprehensive
- compound

Comprehension

A 🧑

1 How did Pip feel about going in the rowing boat for the first time?
2 Explain how Pip ends up in the water, being towed by the whale.

B 🧑

1 In your own words, describe the reaction of Tashtego and Stubb when Pip falls into the water and is caught up in the rope.
2 *Moby-Dick* was written in the nineteenth century and some of the language has changed since then. Look at lines 26–37 and find words or phrases used for the following:
  a 'easy to come by' b 'you' c 'do you understand'

C 👥

1 Do you think Pip was lucky? Explain your answer.
2 Do you think Stubb is a good man? What do you think Stubb will do next time Pip does something wrong?

Stretch zone

Look at the painting at the bottom of page 176. Imagine you are one of the hunters. Describe the action using powerful, descriptive words and a variety of sentence lengths to make the action exciting.

Write Pip's diary

Write the story from Pip's point of view as if you are writing a diary entry. Remember to use:
- a variety of sentence lengths to build up the drama
- Non-Standard, informal English to imitate how Pip would write in his journal
- strong verbs and adjectives to describe the action
- literary and rhetorical devices to increase the impact.

12 Island living

What is it like to live on an island?

> **"No man is an island, entire of itself; every man is a piece of the continent, a part of the main"**
>
> JOHN DONNE

Talk about ...

- Have you visited an island on holiday? Why do you think so many islands have become tourist attractions? How do you think the local people feel about all the tourists who visit?

- If you were stranded on a desert island with just one other person, who would you like that person to be? If you could have one item from home, what would it be? Maybe a luxury, a book, or a pet?

Island quiz

See how many questions you can answer with a partner. If you don't know the answer, have a guess.

1 How many ocean islands in the world are there?
2 How many islands in the ocean, sea and lakes are inhabited by humans?
3 Which is the biggest inhabited island in the world?
4 Which is the most remote island inhabited by people?
5 Which is the largest island in the Caribbean Sea?
6 Which is the second largest island in the Mediterranean Sea?
7 Which young British naturalist and explorer famously visited the Galápagos Islands (Ecuador) on the HMS *Beagle* in 1835?

Word origins

Galápagos (n), comes from an old Spanish word *galápago*, meaning 'tortoise'

- Compare texts on the same theme
- Contribute to group discussion and communicate personal opinions confidently

Which island would you visit?

Islands have captured the human imagination throughout history with their promise of adventure, isolation and discovery. It is no surprise that holidays to islands are very popular – close your eyes and imagine the sand beneath your feet, the salty breeze on your face, and the gentle sound of the lapping waves …

Fernando de Noronha, Brazil

Noronha's main attractions are its unspoilt sandy beaches and stunning tropical landscapes. The surrounding crystal clear water is teeming with rich marine life, including dolphins. To protect this wildlife haven, only a few tourists are allowed to visit the island daily. Hiking along the trails of Jardim Elizabeth or the stunning Esmeralda Coast will leave tourists with wonderful memories.

Crete, Greece

There is so much more to Crete than just beautiful sandy beaches, turquoise sea and lots of sunshine. This fabulous island is famous for its ancient history and Minoan landmarks. The Palace of Knossos, the most important of Crete's sites, contains a number of important archaeological finds.

Lofoten, Norway

With its distinctive scenery of dramatic mountains and peaks, sheltered bays and untouched beaches, there is no other destination like the archipelago of Lofoten. Visitors can enjoy hiking, scuba diving, skiing, fishing and ocean rafting, as well as natural phenomena like the midnight sun and the northern lights above the picturesque fishing villages.

In a group, decide which island you would most like to visit together and why. Think about:

- whether you like to be active on holiday or relax by a pool
- what kind of attractions are important to you, for example:
  - wildlife
  - ancient monuments
  - beach sports
  - fishing
  - shopping
  - nightlife
  - natural phenomena
  - art and culture.
- whether you like to be with lots of other people or somewhere more remote.

Glossary

archaeological relating to the study of human history and prehistory through the excavation of sites and analysis of artefacts

phenomena remarkable person or thing

A story of survival

Read this review of a book which tells the story of a young boy who leaves his home island and returns to find it completely destroyed by a tidal wave.

Terry Pratchett's South Sea adventure is a comic triumph, says Frank Cottrell-Boyce

Nation takes place on a South Sea island in a skewed version of the nineteenth century. As a genre, the desert island adventure story has more than its fair share of masterpieces, including *Robinson Crusoe,*
5 *Treasure Island* and *Lord of the Flies. Nation* sits comfortably alongside them. It tells the story of Mau, a South Sea islander who is about to move from boyhood to manhood via a traditional rite of passage. This involves him being taken to a nearby haunted
10 island and left there to find his own way home. When Mau gets home, however, home has vanished. A tidal wave has washed away his whole society and replaced it with a wrecked survey ship and a well-brought-up young British girl, Daphne.

15 At first these two are wary of each other – Mau is not even sure that Daphne is real – and Pratchett has a lot of fun with their inability to understand each other, and their attempts to hold on to their own cultures. There's a particularly funny and poignant scene in which
20 Daphne invites Mau to tea. Her invitation helpfully includes a map with arrows on it. Mau takes this to mean she wants him to fire arrows at her. She tries to cook scones for him, but the flour is contaminated by dead lobsters. As the potential for misunderstanding and danger mounts, there's an electrifying
25 moment when he suddenly grasps that she means well.

As the days go by, the island fills up with refugees, and both children find themselves having to do things their culture would never allow. The polite, repressed Daphne has to chew meat for an old lady with no teeth. When the growing community
30 comes under threat from raiders, Mau finds to his surprise and

Glossary

tidal wave exceptionally large ocean wave

skewed make biased or distorted in a way that is regarded as inaccurate, unfair or misleading

contaminated made impure by exposure to or addition of a poisonous or polluting substance

repressed restrained or oppressed

horror that he has to lead a people after all. There's a twist that gave me goosepimples of delight: if you read it to your 10-year-olds, they will gasp and giggle.

35 At the same time, you could read it to a conference of philosophy professors and they would learn something. *Nation* has profound, subtle and original things to say about the interplay between tradition and knowledge, faith and questioning. During his initiation ritual, for instance, Mau discovers that the island isn't haunted at all, and that his dad and uncle have already 40 been there and left supplies and a canoe for him. On one level this means the ancient ritual is a piece of empty theatre. In another sense, though, it's a rite of passage that is supposed to teach him self-reliance and courage. In fact, it gives Mau a much more profound knowledge – of how much his dad loves 45 him and how valued he is by his society. Without the theatre of the ghosts, he wouldn't experience the reality of the love.

Terry Pratchett, the author of *Nation*

Book club reviews

Julie says …

Wow. Terry Pratchett always packs a punch but this narrative is loaded with action and powerful messages! He challenges our concept of what society, faith, science and laws mean. He balances humour with sobriety and the result is something unique and truly quite brilliant.

Ervin says …

This was my initiation into Terry Pratchett. I struggled at first with his introductions to the two different societies – the 'civilized' versus the 'primitive' and mythical one. I had trouble putting these concepts together, and the story seemed to develop very slowly. It got better as I got used to his style of writing and I'm pleased I made it to the end.

Hafsa says …

Written from the perspectives of different characters, Nation tells a story that will bring you joy at the same time as it tears your heart out (well, it will if you're a romantic). You will live and breathe every moment with these characters as if they were your own family or loved ones.

Comprehension

1 What genre is the book *Nation*?

2 Give a quotation from the first paragraph that shows that the reviewer Cottrell-Boyce thinks *Nation* will become a classic.

3 Why do Mau and Daphne have a problem in understanding each other?

4 Cottrell-Boyce makes reference to a significant moment in the story where Mau and Daphne's relationship changes. What happens in this significant moment?

5 What does Mau learn about what his father has done for him? How does this make him feel?

1 Describe the characters of Mau and Daphne. For each character, give three ideas and support each idea with evidence from the text.

2 Use the context of the text to work out what the following words and phrases mean:
- rite of passage (line 8)
- wary (line 15)
- poignant (line 19)
- a piece of empty theatre (line 41).

Use a dictionary to check if you are right.

3 Various types of punctuation are used in the text for different reasons. Explain why the following punctuation has been used:
- hyphens (line 13)
- dashes (lines 15–16)
- colon (line 32)
- brackets (Hafsa's book club review).

1 Look at the book club reviews. Which member of the book club do you think is:
- rather sentimental?
- a firm Terry Pratchett fan?
- unlikely to read another of Pratchett's books?

2 After reading the reviews, do you think *Nation* is the sort of book you would enjoy? Why? Why not?

3 What do you think is the sudden and unexpected change in the story or plot?

Stretch zone

Write a short book review of the last book you read. You can use the short extracts from the book club reviews as a model for your writing.

- Write a book review, including typical features
- Use punctuation accurately

Review a book

Write a detailed review of a book that you have read recently. Use the review of *Nation* as a model for your own review and remember to include the following:

- the name of the author, the book title and a one-line summary of the main theme
- a brief description of the plot
- relevant details about the main characters and setting
- what you liked about the book and thought worked well
- a conclusion saying why the book is worth reading and who you think would enjoy it most.

As you write your review, try and include all the punctuation marks listed in the box below.

When you have finished, share your review with the rest of the class.

colon (:) used before a list, example or quotation

hyphen (-) used to join words or parts of words to make compound adjectives ('well-known writer'), compound nouns ('passer-by') or some words with a prefix ('co-ordinate')

dash (–) used to show interruption (often in dialogue), to separate a different idea (or aside) or to emphasize information

semi-colon (;) used to link two closely related independent clauses in one sentence or in a list where items already contain commas

brackets ( ) (or parentheses) used in pairs to add, clarify or explain information, or to add asides, comments or extra details

The wonders of the South Sea: Rapa Nui (or Easter Island), Chile, is home to the *mo'ai*, a series of stone human figures carved to honour the islanders' ancestors between approximately 1250 and 1500 CE

- Read and enjoy poetry
- Work out the meaning of new words

Colourful poetry

Read this poem about a man waking up in the morning.

Island Man

Morning
and Island man wakes up
To the sound of blue surf
In his head
5   The steady breaking and wombing

Wild seabirds
And fishermen pulling out to sea
The sun surfacing defiantly

From the east
10 Of his small emerald island
He always comes back groggily groggily

Comes back to sands
Of a grey metallic soar
To surge of wheels
15 To dull North Circular roar

Muffling muffling
His crumpled pillow waves
Island man heaves himself
Another London day

GRACE NICHOLS

Glossary

North Circular northern
part of the inner ring road
around London

- Discuss how poets play with themes and conventions
- Explain how language features create effects
- Perform poetry confidently
- Write a poem

Comprehension

1 What does Island man hear when he begins to wake up?
2 What does he hear when he is fully awake?
3 Where is Island man from?
4 Where is Island man now?
5 What do you think is the main theme of the poem?

1 What do you think 'wombing' means in this context?
2 Find an example of each of the following literary features:
   - alliteration
   - personification
   - a metaphor (which isn't personification)
   - external rhyme.
3 What effect does the repetition of words 'groggily groggily' and 'muffling muffling' create?
4 What do you notice about the punctuation in the poem? What effect does this have when you read the poem out loud?

1 Which colours are linked to Island man's memories of his original home? Which colour does he connect with London?
2 What colours would you miss from your country? Are there particular colours that remind you of a place, a person or a time in your past? What's your favourite colour? Why?

Write a poem

Imagine a school friend has moved to an English-speaking country such as Australia, the USA, New Zealand or the UK. Write a poem about them. Think of the contrast between where they moved from and the country they live in now. What do you think they would miss the most? Use 'Island Man' as a model for your own poem.

Stretch zone

Practise reading 'Island Man' out loud. Try to memorize the poem so you do not need to keep looking at the words. Recite the poem to a partner.

Language tip
Internal rhyme is the placing of rhyming words within one line of poetry.

For example: 'There was a frog on a log that croaked in the fog.'

External rhyme (or end rhyme) is the placing of rhyming words at the end of lines of poetry.

For example: 'There was a large frog that croaked,
It sat on a leaf and got soaked.'

The number of local people living on many islands, especially remote rural ones, is decreasing. Young people do not want to live in small communities and are moving to the mainland or other countries. What impact do you think this has on the local community? Is it important to maintain a wide range of age groups in a community? If you lived on an island, what would encourage you to stay to live and work there?

- Read and enjoy a playscript
- Recognize the structure and main features of playscripts

Treasure Island

Treasure Island is a story about a 12-year-old boy, Jim Hawkins, who finds a treasure map of an island and then sails to the island to claim the treasure. The story has been adapted into a play. In the scene below, Jim arrives at the island with a group of untrustworthy sailors and quickly realizes he may have made a mistake. He thinks he's alone as the scene starts.

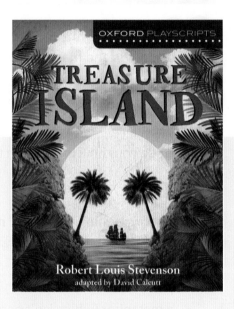

OXFORD PLAYSCRIPTS

TREASURE ISLAND

Robert Louis Stevenson
adapted by David Calcutt

Act III, Scene 3

The chorus enters, keeping back and in shadow. They are now the voices of the island.

	1st voice	But is he? Is he really alone?
	2nd voice	Or is there someone else there?
5	**3rd voice**	Someone, or something else there?
	4th voice	A shadow in the shadows …
	5th voice	A whisper in the leaves …
	6th voice	A figure, flickering amongst the trees.
	Jim (*calls out, looking around him.*)	
10		Who's there?

(*The chorus speaks together.*)

	All	Who's there?
	Jim	Who is it?
	All	Who is it?
15	**Jim**	Who are you?
	All	Who are you?
	Jim	Where are you?

(*Chorus speaks individually.*)

	1st voice	Here.
20	**2nd voice**	Here.
	3rd voice	Here.
	4th voice	Here.
	5th voice	Here.
	6th voice	Here.
25	**Ben Gunn**	(*suddenly appears.*)
		Here, boy!

Learning tip

A **chorus** is a group of actors who do not take part in the action. They speak directly to the audience, commenting on the action taking place on stage.

- Read and enjoy a playscript
- Recognize the structure and main features of playscripts
- Work out the meaning of new words

(*Jim turns, with a cry.*)

	Ben Gunn	Have you come with that ship? That ship, anchored off there. I seen her come in. Have you come with her?
30	**Jim**	Yes …
	Ben Gunn	Is she Flint's ship? Tell me true, boy!
	Jim	No … but there are some of Flint's men aboard …
35	**Ben Gunn**	I knew it! I could smell 'em! And is among them … a man with one leg?
	Jim	You mean Silver?
	Ben Gunn	Yes! Silver! I mean him! Silver! Was you sent by him, boy?
40	**Jim**	No. I want nothing to do with him, or the rest of Flint's men. There are honest men too aboard that ship …
	Ben Gunn	And be you one of them honest men?
	Jim	I hope so …
45	**Ben Gunn**	But you ain't sure, is that it? Well, I'll tell you, boy. You have an honest look about you. So, you tell me, what be honest men doing putting in at this island?
	Jim	We have a map of Flint's treasure …
50	**Ben Gunn**	His map? You have Flint's map?
	Jim	Yes …
	Ben Gunn	And you've come a-looking for his treasure. Come a-looking to dig it up again …
	Jim	That's right …
55	**Ben Gunn**	And he'd take it from you. Silver. He'd take it from you. Is that the right of it?
	Jim	More or less …
60	**Ben Gunn**	I know it is! I know Mr John Silver and his crooked ways. For they was mine, once, they was. I walked his path. But not no more, no. For look what it's brought me to! See where wickedness has brought poor Ben Gunn!

Language tip

Some word groups in English are considered 'feminine'. These include ships and some countries, for example. Ships and boats are referred to as 'she'.

For example: 'I visited my cousin on his yacht – she's a beautiful boat.'

Glossary

crooked dishonest; illegal

187

- Read and enjoy a playscript
- Recognize the structure and main features of playscripts
- Work out the meaning of new words

	Jim	Is that your name?
65	**Ben Gunn**	Ben Gunn, aye, and I haven't spoken to a human soul for three years. None that was living, anyways. And how do I come to be here, eh? Shipwrecked, says you? No, says I. Not shipwrecked. Marooned! Marooned three years gone! Tell me, boy! Answer me
70		true! You wouldn't have any cheese about you, would you?
	Jim	Cheese? No …
75	**Ben Gunn**	I guessed you wouldn't. A piece of cheese, is all I wants. Goats and berries and oysters I have, but no cheese. There's many a long night I've dreamed of cheese – toasted cheese – and then I've woke, and I'm here – and then I've wept to dream again …

(*He sits, forlorn, and appears for the moment to have forgotten Jim.*)

80	**Adult Jim** (*narrates.*)	
85		And he sat on the ground, a ragged, scorched, scarecrow of a man – and I felt such pity for him, so forlorn and desolate he seemed … like a creature from some old tale, the outcast and outlawed king of the island …
	[…]	
	Jim	I promise you, Ben Gunn, if things turn out well for us, and if we ever get away from this island, we'll take you with us.
90	**Ben Gunn**	Them's honest words, lad, honest words from a gentleman. But are they just your words, eh? What about them others aboard? Are they as honest as you?
95	**Jim**	They're all gentlemen. They'll say the same as me.
	Ben Gunn	They will, will they? Well, now, when you see them again, you'll tell them gentlemen – "Here's Ben Gunn," says you, "as sailed with Flint – Ben Gunn three years on this

Glossary

marooned left trapped and alone in an inaccessible place, especially an island

forlorn pitifully sad and abandoned or lonely

scorched burned by flames or heat

scarecrow object made to resemble a human figure, set up to scare birds away from crops

Language tip

Writers sometimes use **irony** to highlight the contrast between expectations and reality. Can you find anything unexpected which might be an example of irony in this extract?

- Read and enjoy a playscript
- Recognize the structure and main features of playscripts

00		island – and he knows the island, he does," says you, "and all her secrets, he knows – all of them, mark you – for he's been here three years and uncovered them all." Do you take my meaning?
05	**Jim**	I'm … not sure …
	Ben Gunn	All of them! Dug right down to her blessed bones, I have! And I wants none of them! You tell your gentlemen, all Ben Gunn wants is his passage home, which he'll pay for like an honest man. That's all, lad. To be off this cursed island. And a piece of cheese. An honest piece of cheese. You makes sure you tell your gentlemen that!
10		
	Jim	I will … if I can ever get back to them …
15	**Ben Gunn**	"If!" says you. "And why that 'if'?" says I. "Cos I have no boat," says you. "But I have," says I.
	Jim	A boat …?
	Ben Gunn	I made it myself! Sticks and goat-skins! You see the white rock? That's where you'll find her. Under the white rock! But you promise me this, boy. If you was to see Silver again, you wouldn't tell him about Ben Gunn, would you? Wild horses wouldn't drag it from you, would they?
20		
25	**Jim**	No.
	Ben Gunn	Your word on it!
	Jim	I give you my word.
	Ben Gunn	You're a good lad.
	(He goes.)	
30	**Adult Jim**	And he was gone, clambering up over the rocks like a goat himself, his figure fading into the shadow, melting back into leaf and tree. And once more, I was alone.

Learning tip

Make sure you know the main **features of a playscript**:

- Playscripts include a list of characters (at the very beginning).

- A playscript may be divided into acts, which are then divided into scenes.

- Each scene usually starts with a description of the setting, followed by the dialogue.

- Dialogue is set out with the character's name on the left and the character's speech (without speech marks) on the right.

- Stage directions for the actors are written in italics and brackets.

A dramatized version of the original novel by ROBERT LOUIS STEVENSON, adapted by DAVID CALCUTT

- Understand how characters are portrayed through speech
- Use implicit and explicit evidence from the text to answer questions
- Perform a playscript

Comprehension

A

1 Why does Jim cry out in line 27?

2 Give one quotation from lines 45–50 which shows that Ben Gunn trusts Jim.

3 Why is Ben Gunn on the island alone?

4 What does Ben Gunn make Jim promise not to do?

B

1 What does Ben Gunn mean in line 60 when he says, 'I walked his path'?

2 Name a language technique used in lines 80–85 to show that Adult Jim remembers feeling sorry for Ben Gunn. Give a quotation to support your answer.

3 Why do you think Ben Gunn often repeats the word 'honest' in this extract? What does it tell us about his character?

4 Why might it be ironic that Ben is referred to as the 'king of the island'? (line 85)

C

1 Do you think the chorus is effective in this extract from *Treasure Island*? Why? Why not?

2 In three years on the island, Ben Gunn has not spoken to a single person nor eaten a single piece of cheese. What would you find most difficult about being stranded on a desert island? How long do you think it would take you to adapt to your new life?

Stage the scene

In small groups, make notes about how you would choose to represent this scene on stage. How would you make it clear that it is taking place on an island? What costumes would you give to the actors? Think also about how you would use scenery, sound effects, lighting and props to build mood and atmosphere.

Perform the play extract in your group. Decide who will take which part. Remember to focus on facial expressions and body language as well as volume and tone of voice to portray your character. When you have fully rehearsed the extract, show your performance to another group and give each other constructive feedback.

The cast of a 2008 British performance of *Treasure Island*

An island for a prince

Read this article about a man who bought a tiny island and turned it into his own country.

Experience: I founded my own country

My father wasn't a king, he was a taxi driver, but I am a prince – Prince Renato II, of the country Pontinha, an island fort on Funchal harbour. It's in Madeira, Portugal, where I grew up. It was discovered in 1419; Captain James Cook has been here,
5 and there are paintings of his visit.

In 1903, the Portuguese government didn't have enough money to build a harbour port, so the king sold the land to a wealthy British family, the Blandys. [...] Fourteen years ago the family decided to sell it for just €25,000. It was of no use to them. But
10 nobody else wanted to buy it either. I met Blandy at a party, and he told me about Pontinha. He asked if I'd like to buy the island. Of course I said yes, but I have no money – I am just an art teacher.

I tried to find some business partners, but they all thought I was crazy to want to buy what is essentially a large rock: it
15 has a small cave, a platform on top, and no electricity or running water. So I sold some of my possessions, put my savings together and bought it. Of course, my wife, my family, my friends – they all thought I was mad.

When the King of Portugal originally sold the island in 1903,
20 he and all the governors signed a document, selling all the "possessions and the dominions" of the island. It means I can do what I want with it – I could start a restaurant, or a cinema, but nobody thought that someone would want to start a country. So that's what I did: I decided that this would no longer be
25 just a rocky outcrop on the port of Funchal, it would be my island, about the size of a one-bedroom house. [...]

I am the police, the gardener, everything. I am whatever I want to be – that's the dream, isn't it? If I decide I want to have a national song, I can choose it, and I can change it any time. The same with
30 my flag – it could be blue today, red tomorrow. Of course, my power is only absolute here, where I am the true sovereign.

RENATO BARROS, in *The Guardian*

Renato Barros

Glossary

fort strong building used as protection against attack
dominions territory of a sovereign or government
outcrop rock formation that is visible above ground
sovereign supreme ruler, especially a king or queen

- Use implicit and explicit evidence from the text to answer questions
- Write from a particular point of view
- Use a model text for own persuasive text

Comprehension

A

1 Who is writing this article?

2 What is the name of his island?

3 Why was the island available to buy?

4 Why does everyone think the writer is 'crazy' for buying the island?

5 What attracts the writer most about the idea of having his own island?

B

1 Explain why the following punctuation marks are used in this text:
- semi-colon (paragraph 1)
- dash (paragraph 2)
- colon (paragraph 3)
- speech marks (paragraph 4)
- question mark (paragraph 5).

2 From the information given, what kind of character is the writer? Give two ideas and support each idea with evidence from the text.

C

1 Would it be a good idea if we all lived on our own tiny individual islands and had access to each other only across the water? What impact would that have on our lifestyles and the natural environment?

2 Would you want to create a bridge (or something similar, like a zip wire) between your island and someone else's?

What would your perfect island be like?

If you could own your own perfect island, what would it be like? Think about and make notes on the following aspects:

- Where is it and what is its name?
- How big is it and what is there?
- Who lives there and where do they live?
- Do you allow tourism?
- What kind of animals are native to your island? Have you introduced any other animals, such as pets?

Illustrate your island on a large sheet of paper. Write notes around your illustration to describe all the features of your island and persuade readers how wonderful it is. You could use Prince Renato's article as a model for ideas.